Becoming Aware of the Logos

Becoming Aware of the Logos
THE WAY OF ST. JOHN THE EVANGELIST

GEORG KÜHLEWIND

Translated by Friedemann and Jeane Schwarzkopf
Edited by Christopher Bamford

LINDISFARNE PRESS

This book is a translation of *Das Gewahrwerden des Logos, Die Wissenschaft des Evangelisten Johannes*, by Georg Kühlewind, published by Verlag Freies Geistesleben.
©1979 Verlag Freies Geistesleben GmbH, Stuttgart.

This edition ©1985 The Lindisfarne Press.

All rights reserved. No part of this book may be reproduced or utilized in any form or by any means, electronic or mechanical, including photocopying, recording or any information or retrieval system, without permission in writing from the publisher.

Published by The Lindisfarne Press
P.O. Box 778, Great Barrington, MA 01230
10 9 8 7 6 5 4 3

Library of Congress Cataloging-in-Publication Data

Kühlewind, Georg.
  Becoming aware of the logos.

  Translation of: Das Gewahrwerden des Logos.
  1. Bible. N.T. John—Theology. 2. Anthroposophy.
I. Title.
BS2615.5.K7513 1985   226'.506   85-23126
ISBN 0-940262-09-6

Printed in the United States of America

ACKNOWLEDGEMENTS

The editor and the publisher would like to thank the following for their help in the preparation of this book: Georg Kühlewind, for his courtesy and generosity of spirit; Dana D. Cummings, for her typography, design, lay-out and many other services, including the typing of an almost indecipherable manuscript; Scott Boxold, who helped the translators at an early stage and made many helpful suggestions; Tadea Dufault Gottlieb and Michael Lipson, who helped the editor in innumerable ways with careful, gifted editing and enthusiastic commitment to the work; and Maria St. Goar, who dedicatedly checked the final manuscript.

The publisher would also like to acknowledge with gratitude the financial assistance received for the publication of this work from numerous persons who wish to remain anonymous.

By the Same Author

Stages of Consciousness, Meditations on The Boundaries of the Soul
(Inner Traditions/Lindisfarne Press, 1984)

Contents

	Preface	11
1	The Presence of the Logos	13
2	The Word in the Beginning	24
3	The Light in the Darkness	33
4	Martyría (Witness)	42
5	The Speaker	58
6	Life	70
7	Spirit	81
8	God's Dwelling: The Temple-City	94
9	The Church	108
10	Cháris and Alétheia	125
11	John	147
12	The Teaching of the Logos and Spiritual Science	165
	Notes	187

A NOTE ON THE TRANSLATION

Translation of this work presented many difficulties, two of which should be noted by the reader.

Firstly, there was the problem of how to properly render the meaning of the German verb, *erkennen* and its corresponding noun form, *das Erkennen*. The word *cognizing* or *cognition* was chosen for the following reason. Whereas the word *kennen* in its everyday usage would have to be translated simply as *knowing*, in the sense of "knowing something," where subject and object are clearly separated, *erkennen* is used differently and has a different connotation. In the first place, rather than "to know," *erkennen* means "to recognize," in the sense of "I recognize my key"; secondly, this "recognition" has a nondualistic connotation, suggesting that subject and object are not divided in the process of cognition. The subject "becomes" the object and thereby comes to know it. To distinguish this kind of nondualistic knowing the word *cognizing* seemed appropriate. To cognize — cognizing, cognition — is not used in everyday language and so calls for special attention from the reader, asking him or her to practice the activity of knowing in order to experience the content of the phrase in which it is used. This may be compared with the way in which "knowing" was used in ancient Greece where, on the entrance to the Temple of Delphi, *Gnothi sauton*, Know thyself was inscribed. It is to this kind of "cognizing" that Kühlewind refers when he uses the word *erkennen*.

Secondly, there was the question of when to capitalize the word *word*. In German, nouns are always capitalized and therefore in the German text the word *das Wort* is also always capitalized. In English, however, capitalization carries more weight. A capitalized word draws attention to itself, setting itself off from the rest of the text. Moreover, capitalization has the effect of objectifying and dualizing the relation between the reader and what is capitalized. We have therefore tended to use the lower case, except in those cases where the Word (upper case) is clearly referred to. Indeed, we have generally used the upper case sparingly. This does not mean, however, that when word (lower case) is used reference to the Word (upper case) is ever necessarily excluded. Far from it. In many cases the reader should realize the immanence of the upper case in the lower: W/w, He/he, It/it. In each case, the reader should ask, Which word, who, what is meant here? What is the relation?

Preface

One need only read the first verses of St. John's Gospel to realize that the text is incomprehensible, even contradictory, to our everyday dialectical consciousness. There are two reasons for this. Firstly, St. John, like the other Evangelists, uses language containing many terms that are unknown to us—terms for experiences that are mostly unknown to contemporary man, as they were indeed to the average man of his own time also. Secondly, the text deals largely with a kind of experience having to do with the cognition of hidden spheres of reality or (to put it another way) with those hidden pre- and super-conscious processes that precede our everyday reflective consciousness and from which this reflective (mirror-) consciousness arises.

Texts like St. John's can only be understood through experiences on the plane of consciousness corresponding to them; yet the "interpretation" emerging from such a meditative understanding can in most cases be supported by philological methods (comparison of passages, etymology etc.). Philology by itself, however, can rarely do justice to the text.

Having occupied myself in this way for many years with St. John's Gospel, I have shared in this volume some of the insights that seem most important to me. No "interpretation" is final, none can exhaust the theme we are dealing with. This is emphasized in my exposition. The themes themselves are all interwoven and difficult to penetrate individually. Some of them therefore appear repeatedly. Thus this book is meant to be an invitation, a challenge to the reader to immerse himself in the source from which John too drew his insight.

Above all, my aim has been to describe the two pillars of St. John's teaching, *alétheia* (truth) and *cháris* (grace), together with the form in which these live on—as eternal truth and eternal goodness—in spiritual science. Nothing is more necessary for human beings today than to grasp these vitally formative ideas.

I wish to thank all the friends who have helped in the work and in the editing of this book, especially Dr. Ruth Moering.

ONE

The Presence of the Logos

> We are only mouth. Who sings the distant heart
> that dwells entire within all things?
> Its great pulse lives in us
> divided into lesser beats. And its great pain,
> like its great joy, is too great for us.
> So we always tear ourselves away again
> and are only mouth.
> But suddenly the great
> heartbeat enters into us invisibly
> and we cry out . . .
> And then are being, change and countenance.
> *Rilke*

To become aware of the Logos is to become aware of the Logos in oneself. This sentence must be understood in all its meanings.

That communication is possible and happens, *that* something is communicated, is the active being of the Logos among human beings. The content of the communication matters little at first. The fact that it happens at all is the presence of the Logos. Without the Logos, there would not be even the attempt to communicate, nor any claim to communication.

Anyone who uses words, speaks — consciously or tacitly —

on the basis of the assumption, even the certainty, that "I am" and "you are," and that truth—knowing—exists. To speak necessarily involves speaking *to* someone. There are no monologues. All monologues *that we know about* are basically dialogues. Whoever engages in a monologue has previously spoken with other speaking beings. When the loneliest person speaks at least one other is present. No one speaks for himself alone. Even the primordial monologue of the Creator immediately turned into a dialogue—even before it was uttered. The Other, the second, was already present in the seed of the primal Word: He was it (John 1.1-3). Therefore the Word is truly the primal beginning. As soon as something moves, to do something or to "think," the Word is there and, with it, the beginning. Even before it appears outwardly, before even (relative) outwardness exists, the Word is already there, before . . . before . . .

When I speak to someone—in my ability to do so—I become, I am. And you—for you I am, and for me you are. The word blossoms between us: cognition, communication, the Logos.

Without cognition neither you nor I would be. Cognition, however, is only possible in freedom. Compulsory cognition, as if by natural law, would not be cognition, but a natural process, analogous to that by which the rosebush brings forth roses. It has to. There can be no argument about it; certainly not with the rosebush, for that is its nature. Nor can you argue with someone about the color of his eyes.

"There is no such thing as cognition" is an impossible statement, which negates itself, as do its variants, "There are things which we cannot cognize" or, generally, "This or that is not cognizable." At the very moment we say that of something we are about to cognize it. The moment we stand at the boundary, the boundary has been crossed.

I conceive, I form the word and let it go, I send it on its way. It floats to you. It is *truth*. That there is truth, that the word exists, *is* truth. And the word lives, is present, not past. It speaks. And at the same time it says, I am there— I am the I-am-there—and *that* is life (*zoé*).[1]

In what follows we shall speak about this floating word; indeed, we have already spoken of it. It itself speaks.

Only I can speak. A wild animal does not speak; it has no choice. It cannot consider its communication and say to itself, "I will not do this now." It must speak, or it cannot. A bird has to give its warning cry, its "signal." Therefore its cry is not a real communication, but a reflex, comparable to a mechanical sequence. With its horizontal vertebrae extending into its head, even if its head is on another level as is the case in the giraffe, the animal "reclines" in the earth's activity. It has not drawn itself upright.

Yet no human being would be upright by nature either. His drawing himself into the vertical posture gives him the world. He stands in it, he does not lie down in it. Thereby he removes himself from it. The word is at once a bridge and a division, a two-edged sword. Only man has expressions for joy and suffering. The animal *is* joy or suffering, is the world.

For man, everything—the world, things, his own body, life and death, as also the word that he speaks—has *meaning*. But the animal *is* all of these.

Man, therefore, has something to communicate. He communicates, shares what he has cognized—even when he lies—and what he has cognized, what is communicable, is the world.

The world consists entirely of words, of communicability. Even the unspeakable becomes therefore communicable. The world is a transparent, *speaking* world. It says: sky-blue, cloud, cedar, frog, pond, rain. But it says this in many languages. Which then is the real word e.g. for the sky? *Himmel, cielo, njebo?* If I want to make myself understood by a Japanese and we know no common language, I will point to the sky, saying "sky," and ask him with a gesture what "that" is called in his language. He understands me and says his word. *What* did he understand, *what* do we have in common? I point to *that*, the sky, and he understands that this *that* is the sky — not the air, not the blue, etc. We understood each other without words: he grasped which *that* I was pointing to and this that was already word, beyond any particular language. He grasped the *real* word, pure understanding, of which every sign, every spoken word, is only an indication. Such wordless understanding makes translation possible. It makes a thing a *thing*. This wordless word is not an outer "name" attached to a thing, it *is* the thing. Someone who does not have the concept "book" will perhaps see only paper. It is the word, i.e. the concept, the function, that makes something into a *thing*. Words, as earthly representatives of the Word, do not *signify* a thing which would exist just as much without its concept, but the thing *becomes* through the word. First the idea of the knife, then the knife, even when it is seen; I see the knife for the first time when its idea dawns in me.

But there are not only *concepts of perceptible things*, "perception words." The following do not designate perceptions gained through the sense-organs, but are "relationship words," as for example: *is* — to be — *as, because, then, also, otherwise, again, enough, strong* etc. "There is nothing in the intellect that has not been first in the senses."

Not a single word, not a concept in this sentence corresponds to its content since none of them originates in a sensory perception.

Relationship words give the real structure, the scaffolding, of our world; and this scaffolding is then filled out with our concepts of perceptible things. They refer to things or phenomena which gain their existence — being *thus*, being *this* — through the word, the concept. Earthly speech is not simply given to man with his physical birth. Through his second birth — the soul's birth — man obtains the ability to speak under the influence of the human environment. Without human beings around him, he would not stand upright. Without this upright posture, his hands would have had to carry his body; they would not be free for the *expression* of the soul, which is born in uttering itself. Pointing, indicating, grasping and wanting to grasp are the first appearance of speech and are, at the same time, the whole of speech. *Whoever* is able to point to something, speaks, and has all that is necessary for speaking: *I, You, That*: Cognition.

A child that cannot point to something cannot learn to speak. The animal does not point; it is not a subject. A single pointing gesture contains all speech within itself. But learning to speak a particular language depends only on the surrounding, not on heredity. The child is not born with an *earthly* language, neither is it gifted more for one language than for another. It can "learn" any language, sometimes even two at the same time. The capacity for language is undifferentiated, not fixed. It is, as it were, primal speech.

One cannot speak of a child learning its mother tongue in the same sense as one speaks of learning in an already thinking human being. Speech is not acquired by explanations, since a child cannot understand explanations. Besides, "relationship words," like prepositions and conjunctions, the true functional categories, described above, cannot be explained. The process is purely intuitive. A word, a gesture —e.g. pointing to something—themselves call forth *understanding* in the child. Only in this way does the child make *that* word, *that* object its own. Intuition, immediate understanding, is here a presupposed capacity, precisely the capacity for the above-mentioned primal speech, for the cognition of "that." No one can learn a language who cannot already speak, who does not already have the undifferentiated predisposition for any language. This is the *primal speech* of which each individual language is a particular crystallized form, to which every real new understanding refers. Earthly words are the vessel or garment for the words of this primal speech, and they arise neither accidentally nor arbitrarily, but by giving up their life. A momentary resurrection occurs in the "floating" word, only to die again immediately afterwards in the "finished" word. With the concretizing of the child's capacity for speech, this original ability to learn a language intuitively also dies away. An adult has to acquire new languages mostly through translation, through words and images.

In learning how to walk, to speak and to think, a subject, gifted with the ability of primal speech, enters corporeal being. This subject connects with the body which becomes its instrument and tool of expression. If the tool is inappropriate, or if for other reasons the connection with the subject is missing, then we say we are dealing with an "abnormal" child. Since "second birth," the birth of the soul, depends on the human "speech" of its surroundings (which means not only actual spoken, audible speech, but also the whole surrounding context of behavior), souls are often born disturbed because of imperfect and, above all, love-less "purposive speech." The child develops according to the way in which its adult environment "speaks," that is, the way in which it expresses its human-ness. Here only the real truth works; hypocrisy cannot help. The way in which his surroundings "speak" has its effect even on the adult, as a text has its effect whether it is understood or not.

In the beginning the speaker is not in the body. He does not identify himself with it. He speaks about his bodily appearance, which the adult world generally sees as "the child," in the second or third person. When the speaker identifies himself with the body he begins to say "I." Then, later, memory (self-reflection) begins. Metaphorically one could say: first he spoke outside the body, with the help of this tool, but now he speaks *out* of it — it speaks *out* of it.

Whoever speaks must be someone.

Whoever can speak is not of this world. *This* world exists *for* and *through* the speaker, through the Logos. Nothing is un-sayable; it is a Logos-world. The speaker or knower is not as such a result of the world he knows. He cannot be conceived as consisting of those elements which he himself has discerned.

Abstract concepts (universals) are primary. Whoever recognizes the common element in many different triangles — big, small, wide-angled, narrow-angled etc. — already has the concept "triangle," by which he recognizes the many varieties of triangle as belonging to the same family. Within ordinary mirrored consciousness — which only reflects already finished, and therefore past, thoughts — there is no reality that corresponds to the universals. The universals are not a reality of *this* world; to this extent the nominalists were correct. Only on the intuitive plane, in the sphere of life, of still-fluid thinking, are universals real. This is also true for meditative texts.² To someone who does not understand them they remain abstract, i.e. not experienced. Similarly with Aristotle's Categories or "relationship words" like prepositions and conjunctions. These do not name a sense-reality, but "carry" the whole sensory world: e.g. Being, Relation, Space, Activity, etc.

We cannot say what speech, what speaking is. Every explanation presupposes that we already know it. Even the question presupposes it. *That* is speech.

Speech is a reality arising and appearing between at least two human beings. A later monologue still testifies to the inner duality of the monologist. If the human were altogether identical with himself, he would neither speak nor think for himself. The cognizer, the "higher" man, is not the same as the earthly man; the speaker is not the same as the "instinctual" man. A monologue is a dialogue between the two. Speech is not man-made. Without speech man is not man. Therefore man could not possibly have "created" the first language. To create already implies speech — *is* speech. Speech, the word, makes human beings human. Even a particular language is so powerful a "thought" that a human being could never bring it forth. We can construct simplified languages on the pattern of those already being spoken. But how could we do this without the first language? Such a thought is a contradiction itself; it is "unthinkable."

Logos is not word, law, sense, reason, measure, etc. It is everything that makes these possible: a *common relationship to the world*, a common world. It is the connecting element. A person says, on my word, I give you my word, and whoever does not keep his word breaks the connection. Nor is the word we have "given" necessarily a spoken word.

The Logos lives in human beings and in the world: inside and outside. Inside and outside are in turn determined by the Logos, for they exist for and through cognition. But, for the Logos, neither the one nor the other is valid. The Logos is neither inside nor outside: It is. The world speaks: *this, that*. Man hears it and is capable of perceiving the speaking itself, which (or who) makes *this* and *that* into *this* and *that*. The Logos is invisible, imperceptible to the senses. It is the invisible one; it is as invisible as the speaker in man: you do not see him either. For the speaker in man is not mouth, tongue, face, head, hand, etc. These are his means of expression, he moves them. All speaking is movement: movement for the sake of expression. Even no movement — silence — can become speech.

Things, the outer world — in their being-that, being-so, being-there — *are* speech; "relationship words" likewise. Since everything is speech, everything speaks to him who can listen. Man is capable not only of hearing what is spoken, but of perceiving speaking itself. This is difficult for him, because he is occupied with *this* and *that*, with what is spoken, and therefore he lives in the past of speech: he has not yet realized its presence. But man can become aware of speaking. The Logos within him can awaken to self-consciousness, "for he became flesh." Now man, who had earlier been "spoken," himself becomes the speaker.

The Logos is not alive in contemporary languages, and has not been for a long time. These languages are word-languages, i.e. every word "means" something once and for all. They are not appropriate to express life or presence directly, but only indirectly as signals for the wordless word.

21

True thinking, improvisation (when one does not know in advance what one is going to think — a rare achievement), *lives* beyond word-languages. Once thinking and speaking were united, as they still are today for the child. Living thinking must penetrate solidified, dead language: this is the resurrection of language. As long as sun, moon, stars and nature-phenomena were transparent for man — garments of the spirit — they were truly experienced and honored as divine beings. *While* he was experiencing them, man still heard the word which "created" them and gave them their existence as sun, moon and stars. He heard the *word* that they were, for they said to man: sun, moon, star. But then they became dark, as they did for Abraham for example. Abraham had to seek the one who made them sun and moon, but who did not *speak* through them any more — the invisible one, who now *was* not sun and moon, but guaranteed the being of *all* of them. This guarantor was the Logos in its garment and appearance as the God of a people and of nature — Jehovah — who could once be reached through the sun and moon, because he made them sun and moon. The Logos is the One God, or the One God's countenance through which the One shows himself to man, looks upon man — veiled, or, at times, face to face.[3] This is why the Logos-religion, the essential, living Christianity, is the universal human religion. The revelation of the Logos in an earthly, human form is the second permeation of man by the Logos (Gen. 2.7) To understand this revelation, to become aware of it, means that man perceives the cognizer and the speaker within himself.

At the first creation of man (Gen. 1.27), God "speaks" man and speaks to him at the same time. This is depicted by Michelangelo[4] in painting's silent language. God *points* to man, and thus creates him, while man responds to God's pointing gesture. Shyly and insecurely, man points to God, to the finger which points firmly at him. The two pointing fingers almost touch; God and man look at each other. The existence of man begins this primal dialogue. *This is man.* The word hovers between them in their pointing and looking. The outer signs, face and hand, point to its real being. Yes, they point.

Throughout the ages the Logos was seen outside man in different forms, as light, as sun, as the illuminating element of the universe, as a person. In the Hebrew religion, it becomes invisible, and sometimes even the expression "God's word" is used.[5] In Christianity, the word moves to the center.

The epiphany of the Logos—his appearance amongst men—is not really possible; real knowing of the Logos is prevented as long as it is seen from outside. Because *cognizing* remains unrealized and unexperienced, one cannot cognize. Cognizing in the deepest depths means simultaneous identity and distinction of I and world, and this occurs only for an "I." Therefore, to become aware of the Logos is to become aware of the inner light, the light of the word. This does not happen anywhere or at any time. Yet it is also true self-consciousness, by which the non-cognizing element, ego-consciousness, recedes. The speaker first reveals himself in human beings in the process of thinking. The intuition of the Logos is simultaneously the intuition of the inner logos. Man awakens in the word. The invisible I-am-the-I-am-there—the living, present God—*becomes* present in and through man.

TWO

The Word in the Beginning

> To keep silent. Who has kept more
>   silent inwardly
> touches the roots of speech.
> Some day each sprung syllable
> will be for him a victory
>
> over what is not silent in silence,
> over mocking evil;
> that he may untie himself without a trace
> the word was shown to him.
> Rilke

The world speaks. Before all else, it says speaking itself. Or does speaking say the world?

What speaks in things, in the world, and the fact that what speaks is a language, has been realized only very late. This was the sign that *the times have been fulfilled*. Greater history has ended: it is the end of times. Now comes *the* time. History was the history of the descent of the Logos. That he was spoken of by *this* name was the sign. Becoming aware of the Logos puts an end to greater history. From now on humanity either continues history — or does not. The decline[6] is on, and, as various forms and traditions testify, humanity *knows* of it.

What does it mean, it knows of it? What does it mean that we always knew about it?

Humanity awaited this moment—this last event. Words of inwardness arise—conscience, thinking, consciousness etc.—and, above all, the idea of the Logos. These are the ideas of the Ram,[7] Aries, who, with his head turned back in a distant, premonitory gesture of the consciousness soul, gazes upon his "past" consciousness, upon himself, his own consciousness.

"The soul partakes of the Logos which grows out of itself."[8] At the end of the great decline the Logos forms within the soul the living place of the world, of what is new and has the capacity for primal beginning. The first, primal beginning was the Logos becoming aware of itself.

Once one has become aware of this element which communicates everything, makes everything accessible to man, and which also constitutes the essence of the world (and for this reason makes it accessible to man), the question arises of the "where" and "when" of the Logos—although not in a spatio-temporal sense. Whence does it come? Since every "thing" that has come into being presupposes the Logos, we discover upon reflection we have to look "back" to the first beginning. If we want to see the origin of the Logos, which is the source of everything, we have to penetrate right down to nothing, to the very beginning. It is the Logos itself, indeed, that makes possible this sight that penetrates back to the primal beginning. The very first sentence of the Prologue (John 1.1) affirms this too: man can see right back to the first beginning. He can see the first beginning and the Logos. Thus the reader is given a task: reproduce this gesture, or the text has no meaning for you. The text exhorts us to do as the one who wrote it down. It says: seeing the first beginning, one sees the Logos there. Hence the reader is expected to do the same. The Logos is the first-born of creation (Col. 1.15; Rev. 3.14); nothing can have come into being before it. As soon as the Creator moves out of His immobility, steps out of his silence, with the first movement, the Logos is there; even before the first gesture occurs, before the first word sounds, *the* word is already present in the Creator. Since that moment, all true speech speaks out of the same first beginning.

The Creator gives up his immobility, his stillness, and points — through the Word — to creation. In pointing with the word, he shows himself, and is revealed. This is the primal revelation, creation itself. Thereby HE — HE who is who he is — becomes the one who reveals himself. He becomes that: what and who he was before; and there was no before. He creates the one to whom he shows himself, and creates showing as such: the Word, the Logos. The Father has no secrets from the Son, for the Creator himself *becomes* through the first creation, the Logos. "For the Father loveth the Son and sheweth him all things that himself doeth" (John 5.20). It cannot be otherwise, since what he does is done through the Logos, and he himself *becomes*, through and for the Logos, He HE and every one of his movements is Logos.

> "Amen, Amen, I say unto you, the Son can do nothing of himself, but what he seeth the Father do: for what things soever he doeth, these also doeth the Son likewise. For the Father loveth the Son, and sheweth him all things that himself doeth: and he will shew him greater works than these, that ye may marvel. For as the Father raiseth up the dead, and quickeneth them; even so the son quickeneth whom he will. For the Father judgeth no man, but hath

> committed all judgment unto the Son: That all men should honour the Son, even as they honour the Father. He that honoureth not the Son, honoureth not the Father which hath sent him. Amen, amen I say unto you, He that heareth my word, and believeth on him that sent me, hath everlasting life, and shall not come into condemnation; but is passed from death unto life. Amen, amen, I say unto you, The hour is coming, and now is, when the dead shall hear the voice of the Son of God: and they that hear shall live. For as the Father hath life in himself; so hath he given to the Son to have life in himself." (John 5.19-26)

The Logos is with him and he is the Logos. It is his countenance, what can be seen of him, what looks and is legible, what "speaks." The Logos is what utters creation and the creature, addressing it simultaneously, and thereby creating light, earth, heaven and man. And it is, it, the Logos, whom the first human couple hear after the fall, God's voice, from which they want to hide (Gen. 3.8).

Resounding, the first monologue ceases to be a monologue.

The primal beginning *is* the Logos. But for something to move at all — humanly speaking, for someone to will something out of himself — for something to *be* that is not, love is needed. That, indeed, *is* love — the love for something that does not yet exist. Where there is truly primal beginning is love; and without the capacity for primal beginning there is no love. For primal beginning means there is no "why" and no "in order to." Therefore love lives behind *all* cognizing — since that too is a first beginning. Without love human cognizing could not penetrate the untransparent and inexplicable "relationship words" through the darkness which separates us from the world of perception and our fellowmen. Cognizing and speaking rest on the unshaken and unshakeable trust that we live in a Logos world—a cognizable world—and that another human being understands us despite the darkness of our words which we cannot see through, because we have not made it. Is not this darkness there, perhaps, in order to make love necessary, to call it forth—so to speak—out of ourselves? In order that love might bridge non-understanding and thereby *become*?

John saw this Logos, this primal beginning. As we would say today, he conceived these ideas. He did not consider creation, the sky and the earth. If he had, his Prologue would not have witnessed the primal beginning; it would have been like the beginning of the Old Testament. But John turned his gaze directly on the Logos; he saw the primal beginning and experienced that one cannot reach back *before* it: "Before Abraham was, I am" (John 8.58)—in the present, because one cannot say: the Logos *was*.

Every account of the beginning is burdened with the contradiction: How can we know about it, since, after all, we were not present when it happened? This paradox afflicts every creation story and is resolved for the first time in John's opening sentences. For John refers only to the Logos. In all earlier accounts of creation the Logos remained the unnoticed element—and yet everything that was seen in the beginning was seen and became by means of the Logos. The Logos was both the unperceived background of created beings in the "beginning" and also the unnoticed means of the *reporting*. Through the perceiving of the Logos *in* the primal beginning and *as* the primal beginning the third contradiction was also resolved for mankind: the word, which today is *with man*, and which he can see, the same was in the beginning (in "principle," i.e. in the primal beginning), so that man can know and report it. The bridge between

28

the first beginning and man is the Logos. It was "present." It was the first beginning. Man does not have to be there in his present form: the Logos in him allows him to look back to the origin of the Logos. Therefore no foreign element, nothing unconsidered, remains in John's account. The Logos showed itself, was finally revealed. The one who was *before* all, was shown to man last of all.

Even the primal beginning itself arose through the Logos, who was "with" God, i.e. in the beginning his face was turned toward God as it was later turned toward the creature, toward man. God became God through the Logos. Therefore St. John says not only *bara* (1.Gen. 1.1), "created" (in the sense of "contemplating," "thinking"), not only "and God *said*" (which implies the existence of the Logos), but in revolutionary fashion he also sets the Logos itself in the beginning. Logos, God and primal beginning are for him three united beings in the primal beginning (John 1.2).

The Logos was in the primal beginning "with" God, but was still far from being "with" man, who did not yet see the Logos, did not see his own cognizing. For this to happen, the Logos had to become flesh and had to enter into man. The Prologue describes this path of the Logos from God to man, and so condenses the entire pre-history of Christianity. At bottom, all traditions, not only that of the Old Testament, describe the stages and steps of this path.

Today, awareness of the Logos is the bridge to the experience of the so-called spiritual world. Other ways of "perceiving" avoid the Logos, and remain outside it. They provide "something," but not what makes it something. Today virtually everyone can approach this Logos element — at least its concept can be grasped dialectically. And this self-illuminating concept leads one to new ideal depths and heights. The Logos idea is pure at every stage and directs itself to the spiritual activity of its own conception. It points to itself, reveals *itself* and not something else. For this reason, St. John directs his spiritual gaze to the Word.

The intuition of the Logos is a whole worldview in the sense of a way of looking at the world. To one who realizes it, it gives the certainty of immortality. For it is the one who is present in man, not his past-consciousness, which is occupied with what has already been thought and perceived, who reaches this intuition. Even *nothing* is still a representation, which I fear to become. This is the experience: everything exists through the Logos; I too am through the Logos. Fear of death derives from the feeling of being identical with the body. Past-consciousness relies on this body, because the body is necessary for this kind of consciousness. The intuition of the Logos, being simultaneously the intuition of the "inner" Logos, frees consciousness from its identity with the body. No speculation brings this certainty, for speculation uses the physical body. Only the intuition of thought is body-free, is caused by nothing yet causes all: such is the primal beginning. In contemplation one tries to "hold" intuition, to extend it in time, otherwise the experience is but an ephemeral flash of lightning. The seed of resurrection and of the concept of the resurrection is laid down with John's very first sentence. Much is "mirrored" in the soul whose "original" seems to be in the phenomenal world. But the activity of "mirroring" does not derive from the mirrored world. This capacity of being a pure mirror is the soul's point of origin: it is the seed and root of the spirit in the soul. Because this point is the source, no reflection can make it visible. Personal difficulties, suffering and sadness are healed only if the soul reaches the original element of *consciousness*, which none of these can touch, the eternal point, to which all this is foreign, but from which everything receives its sense and meaning as suffering, sadness and illness. All suffering, illness and sadness demonstrate the distance of this point from the place where suffering, illness and sadness are felt. At this point, the word is born in man: the principle, the primal beginning of healing. For all suffering is caused by forgetting the word, by our failure to become aware of it. This failure is cognitive naiveté: that worldview which allows no reality to cognition, to the Logos, even though all reality is recognized through cognition. As far as this goes, materialism and traditional spiritualism are in agreement with each other. They are only apparently contradictory. Basically, they represent the same disease of the human spirit, while healing lies in the primal beginning, in the intuition of the Logos. The Logos teaching is a cognitive teaching, the only possible one, since the primal reality is cognition. Therefore John, in his first sentences, immediately indicates the source which makes possible the healing of the most bitter human sickness: blindness and deafness to the Logos, to God's voice—from whom, after the fall, the first couple wanted to hide, and which thereafter disappeared from men into its concealment. St. John's text points the way to what it announces; and along this way our common blindness is healed. Man can turn back to the primal beginning. With the Gospel's first sentences, what was hidden to man for aeons comes into the open, into *alétheia*,[9] into truth:

"In the beginning was the Logos, and the Logos was with God, and God was the Logos (1).

The same was in the beginning with God (2).

All things became through it, and without it not one thing has become that became (3).

In it was life, and the life was the light of men (4);

31

and the light appears in the darkness; and the darkness has not received it into itself (5).

There came a man, sent from God, whose name is John (6).

The same came for a witness, that he might bear witness of the light, in order that all men through him might believe (7).

He was not the light, but was sent to bear witness of the light (8).

It was the true light, that illuminates the whole man, coming into the world (9).

It was in the world, and the world became through it, and the world did not know it (10).

It came into individual being, and individual beings have not received it (11).

But to those who received it, to those who believed in its name, it gave the ability to become children of God (12);

who were born, not of blood, nor of the will of the flesh, nor of the will of man, but of God (13).

And the Logos became flesh, and made his tent within us, and we have seen his radiance, as the radiance of the self-born (*monógenes*, born of one) son of the father, full of grace and truth (14)."[10]

THREE

The Light in the Darkness

> Earth, is not this what you want:
> *invisibly* to rise within us? —
> Is it not your dream to be one day invisible? —
> Earth: invisible!
> What is your urgent command,
>   if not transformation?
> Earth, dear Earth, I will.
>
> *Rilke*

In contemplation, the inner eye turns toward the Logos and beholds the beginning, the union of God and Logos in the beginning, when the Logos is turned toward God. Although *prós* in the Greek text may indeed be translated "with" as it usually is — viz. "the same was *with* God in the beginning" — it has, however, the distinct connotation of "to," "toward," i.e. turned towards him. The later theme of "turning" derives its meaning from this original state.[11]

St. John's gaze now shifts to the present and summarizes the fundamental teaching on cognition in a single brief sentence: all is language, speech or speaks itself. Through the metamorphoses of the Logos, which is life-light, contact with the darkness comes about. This second essential point follows the opening theme of "the Logos in the primal beginning." The light appears in the darkness, and the

33

darkness has not received it into itself. Here the text pauses, interrupts the flow of the description of the descent, and the "interpolation" about John the Baptist follows. We shall know more of its meaning before we return to the destiny of the Logos-Light. The Prologue then culminates with "and we have seen his glory . . ." (John 1.14). After the description of the relationships of the Logos with the light, the text returns, in significant phrases, to the glory and radiance of the Logos.

These two turning points are emphasized by the grammatical form. Apart from the verb "illuminates" in the subordinate clause (John 1.9), which is also related to the light, only a single verb in the entire Prologue is in the present tense, all others are in the past tense. This is the verb "appears." Equally emphatic is the phrase, "and *we* saw," the only personal moment in the Prologue, all other predicates being in the third person. Light indeed must be spoken of in the present tense, for it, like the I am (John 8.58), cannot be mentioned in the past tense. In a true text, form and inner meaning originate from *one* source, and are not accidental. The personal pronoun at the climax of the Prologue, coming after that beginning and those themes, is a very emphatic sign. For many people the three themes—the Logos in the primal beginning, the light in the darkness, and man's beholding of the Son's radiance (glory)—have become three stumbling blocks which scandalize and offend. For traditional people it is a monstrous thought that the light appears in the darkness and shines. It means that the darkness is not absolute evil, but *serves*, perhaps for the calling forth of love, the becoming aware of the light, so that the light may receive its idea through man and become true light. Only in combination with its idea is everything

THE LIGHT IN THE DARKNESS

what it is. The unperceived light, not grasped as idea, is not yet the *true* light of man, which appears at first only in a few people. True light[12] is fully idea, inner experience. It is nothing perceived through the senses, because the senses perceive only what has already been lit. The theme of "the light in the darkness," recurs in that the Saviour, expected from time immemorial, does not come to the nobility, the rulers and the scribes, but rather to the poor, the sick, the sinners. Thus he does end as an earthly ruler, but rather dies a shameful death, far from the stage of history on an otherwise insignificant patch of earth. The world hardly notices it. The light which has come into the world bears no resemblance to the light of pre-Christian tradition. It is the light in the darkness: for tradition, a revolutionary and heretical theme.

Even more shattering is the idea of the God who, to realize his path into darkness, became flesh. The darkness in man, the "prince of this world" in the soul, revolts against this theme. Even today, the climax of the Prologue has not yet been digested by mankind. For "we saw his radiance," or glory, means that because of the Logos living in him, man is capable of "seeing" the Son of God, i.e. God's countenance. Only Dante — who is also heretical — sees this countenance at the end of his *Commedia*. Nothing is hidden anymore, one can enter into the secrets of God. How far removed from this insight had theology already become in the Middle Ages! Even Thomas Aquinas (in a kind of *ignorabimus* which sounds out through many centuries in various forms) teaches that human cognition is limited when directed towards the divine. St. John stands in direct contradiction to this theology as well as to Judaism, in which the hope of cognition had been extinguished.

35

Darkness *is*, because it sees the light as darkness — as something else — and not as light.[13] If the darkness had been the light as light, then it would have "received it into itself," and the darkness itself would have become light. Darkness exists only for and through the light — the light of cognition — because "darkness" is already cognized darkness; and yet the fact that darkness seems to be darkness in spite of this — *that* is darkness.

Humanity lives in darkness in so far as it does not receive the true self-illuminating light into itself.[14] The middle epoch of the history of the world is characterized by the efforts of the teachers and leaders of humanity to make human beings understand the light-character of the world. Hence the divine world is portrayed by means of visual experiences, as a light. This portrayal itself is a powerful means of instruction. Man needs a picture. But whoever can distinguish between picture and reality is on the way to becoming an I.

In the human being light and darkness are mixed. Man consists of a higher light-man, the bearer of cognition, and of a non-cognizing "lower" man. Both are needed for cognition. Light must appear against the background of darkness in order to be perceived, i.e. for true cognition to occur. This mixture or entanglement is the fall. The eyes are opened. But they are not opened in true cognition, because the eye saw, the hand took hold of, what was *already* cognized. Thereby the light hid from man and a darkening took place. This was no cognitive act, but an "eating." It was the first eating of this kind which was not at the same time cognition — the first sign of pleasure (Gen. 3.6), of separateness. Therefore everything that is not turned toward cognition or based on cognition is temptation. For millenia, mankind has tried to compensate for this error with a particular kind of "eating," *cognizing* eating—for example, Communion in Christianity. The first human couple is changed; passive cognition is given to them. They become knowers of good and evil through their deed—which is already prepared for them by their being forbidden to eat from the tree in the midst of the garden. Only *afterwards* does the human being become a cognizer of good and evil: to this day that is our weak point. Good and evil have become mixed, like light and darkness. With the fall, the *simultaneous* history of the descent of man and the Logos begins. The process of becoming human begins at the same time as the work of redemption which reveals its coming among men with the *etheasámetha*—"we saw."

Man's communion with God is the word, his capacity for the word: this is his participation in the Logos. Therefore the text of the Prologue returns in its description of the last step of the Logos from the "light" to the "word." What was in the primal beginning, God's Logos, not the light, becomes flesh. Following the fall, through which his eyes were opened, man wants to avoid God's voice and hide himself from God's face, the Logos (Gen. 3.8). Man, represented by John, now turns from the experience of sight to the word. This world-historical turning is prepared for, as in a prelude, by the Hebrew religion. Moses rejects any attempt to portray God or make him visible. What Moses and his people hear is God's voice and speech (Num. 4.12). The word is the more original element. In it man awakens. It is the word that makes possible man's self-cognizing being. He cognizes even the light itself through the word—word light—just as the light was created through the Word.

Behind what is seen there can be something else. What is seen can be symbol. The word itself speaks and expresses itself. Whoever utters it becomes a Self. Continuing this sequence, under the same zodiacal sign, the last act of the last epiphany takes place, the perfect entrance into invisibility, ascension, and following it, a prelude of the third age: Pentecost, a resounding word-filled event. The Spirit is all word, not sight. Already before the age of the Spirit — i.e. of the capacity to speak the truth purely from within — "we walk by faith," in inner certainty, "not by sight" (2.Cor. 5.7). By the Logos entering and dwelling in humanity, man achieves new sight. To perceive the radiance, the glory, is an inner act of seeing — some translations say, not incorrectly, "teaching" instead of "glory" or "radiance" — and this now replaces earlier "outer" seeing, which also could perceive the Logos in the world.

The second age, the age of history under divine guidance, begins with the fall, with the mixture of light and darkness, good and evil; its positive aspect is that the light appears in the darkness. During this age pedagogy "develops," accompanying the descent of human consciousness. Guiding it in particular ways, it prevents its total darkening. This pedagogy "remembers," as it were, its origin in the light so that the possibility of an independent ascent might be preserved. One human figure, who works in the spirit of this pedagogy, is the witness to the light, a "child of God," John the Baptist. Only the third epoch can bring about the final answer. Spiritually this begins with the incarnation of the Logos. John the Baptist and John the Evangelist stand at either side of the boundary between the two epochs and reach their hands across the border. The one points to the Son, whom he sees with the eyes of old wisdom, the other shows by his work how to cognize him through a new form of consciousness, which has gone *through* the darkening, through death, and for which the light in the darkness has become cognizable.

This is the consciousness which penetrates through *létheia* — the forgetting, the hiddenness, the loss of light — into the age of the Spirit. There are many connections between the two Johns. Naturally, the two ages are not sharply separated. Nevertheless, may one may say that the seed of the third age was sown through the event in Palestine about 2,000 years ago, and that this event was humanly represented and described by St. John the Evangelist. But this annunciation is made in the name of "light in the darkness." *It is* the light in the darkness. To this day his teaching is still the light in the darkness in us — because the pre-Christian world-view survives, even in the form of an anti-Christian attitude, and yet just *this* darkness is the soil in which the new light can grow.

The Prologue is organized according to these three spiritual epochs. With the second, the drama enters the human sphere with the words, "the light of men" — a light common to all men — and it continues through John the Baptist to its culmination: the possibility of becoming a child of God. *Then*, yet another step is made: "And the Logos became flesh." Thus the text characterizes the third age, the age of the Spirit, through the *etheasámetha* (we saw) and the two gifts which man can receive through the Logos: *cháris* and *alétheia*, grace and truth. This third epoch is set off from the epoch of the children of God by the word "and": ". . . and the Logos became flesh." *"And"* here means a new step. John states it clearly in his first Epistle: "Beloved, now we are the children of God, and it did not yet appear what we shall be: but we know that, when it shall appear, we shall be like him; for we shall see him as he is" (1.John

3.2). This new state, beyond being a child of God, is realized through seeing the Son, as we read about in the Prologue and the Epistles of Paul to the Corinthians (1.Cor. 13.12; 2.Cor. 3.18).[15]

The Logos appears thrice in the world. First, in the sphere of the divine (John 1.1-2). Then, as creative principle (John 1.3-4), which at the same time allows man to cognize creation. This is the light of men. But the light is not seen (John 1.5). Instead the last witness to the light appears (John 1.6-8), who has taken it up as a child of God. For the children of God, the light is still a foreign, supra-worldly element. Finally, in the third phase, the Logos enters his own tent — comes into his own — and lives in man, amongst men, enabling them to become, beyond children of God, radiating centers of grace and truth (John 1.16-17). They experience the Logos. John the Baptist appears, not just by interpolation, but as part of a coherent progression. In contemplation, the Evangelist sees the refusal of the light, his inner sight seeks the point of departure for further development, and the figure of the witness is found. (A similar movement occurs in the third chapter: Nicodemus has not quite been able to understand the transition from the former transcendence to the new immanence, from man's earlier spiritual make-up to the new stage.) Following this, the text returns — seemingly without cause — to the Baptist, who completely understood the situation of the world (John 3.27-36). Lingering in this way over the figure of the Baptist strengthens the Evangelist's contemplation so that he can grasp and describe the further approach of the light (John 1.9-13). Where the Evangelist meets with incomprehension he looks toward and points to the Baptist, as he does for example for Nicodemus. In other words: we too must understand as John the Baptist did.

THE LIGHT IN THE DARKNESS

The text makes a coherent distinction between "was" and "has become." "Was"—*én*—stands for all that is supra-earthly, all spiritual being; "has become"—*egéneto*—stands for all that has been created, that does not derive from the primal beginning. Thus verses 1 and 2 are entirely under the sign of the heavenly. The creation of "all" is described thrice with the verb *gígnomai*, from which *egéneto* derives (3). This word contains the root "gen," meaning birth, genus, origin, "genesis." Life and light "were" (4). The Baptist "has become" (6). The true light (9,10) "was," the world became through it. But in the end even the Logos "became" flesh (14). It became the one who has become by giving up its eternal nature. And this gives man his new ability, his third phase. Since the Word now dwells within him, man can see the light—the light which is the radiance of the Logos—without tearing his consciousness from the body and without changing the plane of his consciousness so abruptly as to lose his connection with everyday-consciousness, as he had to previously when the human body was left behind by the cognitive principle during the spiritual experience.

Since the Logos entered the flesh, the light can "be seen in the flesh," the cognizer remains in the body. The heavens have drawn near, the light can really shine and appear in the body's darkness. The darkness—the non-cognizing, the earthly—receives the light into itself and is gradually transformed by it into a figure of light.

FOUR
Martyría (Witness)

> If drinking is bitter become wine.
> *Rilke*

A theme like "the light in the darkness" can neither be translated nor explained. One may look at it from ever new view-points, but all of these together will never exhaust its meaning. The sense is inexhaustible because the theme is alive. Really, all one can do is repeat: "The light appears in the darkness."

The darkness is what does *not* receive the light into itself. St. John's inner gaze moves to the figure of the Baptist, the first witness to the light, and then returns to the idea of the true light, that needs no witnesses, but bears witness of itself (John 8, 14).

The light appears in the darkness. St. John can now turn to the new possibility of cognition.[16] Cognition can only occur if a part of man's living nature, which one may describe, at least occasionally, as "the living man" or "the life," detaches and frees itself from the physical body, which it keeps alive. Pre-Christian methods of initiation produced liberation of this kind in various ways. In the most extreme case the novice was placed into a deep sleep similar to death. When recalled to waking consciousness after about three and a half days in that state, he had become witness to the divine-spiritual world, the world of cognition. In this kind of initiation, which was characterized by sudden, unconsciously experienced changes and reversals of consciousness, everyday-consciousness was extinguished.

For present day humanity this process is no longer possible or necessary. The life-principle in human beings has become relatively free. Following the evolutionary development of the human nervous system and the process of death implicit in it, man has now attained a "life" free for autonomous cognition. Starting from his everyday-consciousness he can now, by his own effort, attain a more perfectly cognizing consciousness. Since this process can only occur by means of inner soul-spiritual gestures and without the help of external measures, it corresponds to "baptism by the spirit."

The type of baptism offered by John implies an intermediate kind of consciousness-experience. It consisted of the complete submersion of a person in water to the point of losing consciousness — i.e. long enough to bring about the partial separation of a man's life-principle from his physical body. It was not a symbolic act. Where the Baptist baptized there was "plenty of water" (John 3.23). Whoever underwent this baptism, following the guidance or instruction previously given by the Baptist, experienced certain spiritual realities to which he could then bear witness himself. This "gentler" procedure prepared the way for the method of the third phase, in which one "remained in the body," experienced the light in the darkness and prepared for the birth of earthly-spiritual love. Being *in* the body is a precondition for the birth of this love.

From this perspective the theme of the Baptist in the Prologue gains new meaning. The figure of the Baptist points towards something still greater: *martyría*, testimony, witness. To witness through the Word is to act in the spirit of "turning to the Word." The word "witness" should not be taken lightly. It bears weight. "*Martyría*" is not merely an ability to report something, but to report and describe in such a way that one's testimony convinces men directly, and allows them to believe — "that all through him might believe" (John 1.7). It was apparently not easy to find false witnesses who were nevertheless convincing (Matt. 26.59-61; Mark 14.55-56). That the sort of witnessing meant here was a special ability, a gift, becomes clear particularly through John's use of the word in the Apocalypse (Rev. 1.2; to *have the power of witnessing*: Rev. 6.9; 12.17; 19.1; further Rev. 1.9; 12.11; Acts 4.33).

The word *martyría* (verb, *martyreîn*) is related to "remembering." It suggests older stages of consciousness, when a human being could be reminded of what he really knew. This idea still echoes in Plato's theory of *anámnesis*, or "unforgetting." To be "reminded" in this way remained valid and necessary until the coming of the epoch of *alétheia*, when "un-hiddenness" became accessible to man.

The text emphasizes the difference between what the Baptist does and what the possibility of the third epoch, the epoch of *alétheia*, makes possible. The Baptist bears witness of the light, but he is not the light (John 1.8). The *Logos*, however, becomes flesh and dwells in man. With his word, the Baptist bears witness to the light. Through his baptism, appropriate witnesses were awakened, ones who could testify to what he taught.

What did the Baptist know? His teaching, described in

the synoptic Gospels more from the point of view of his relationship to men, appears in the Fourth Gospel in its deeper sense. Based on this, we may say that he knew all that was necessary to understand the Son's being. Therefore we read in the synoptic Gospels that the Lord, at the beginning of his ministry, uses the same themes, even the same phrases, that sounded earlier from the mouth of the Baptist: "Repent"—change your consciousness—"for the kingdom of heaven is at hand" (Matt. 4.17; 3.2; Mark 1.15; 1.4). St. John's Gospel reverses this relation. What the Lord says to Nicodemus sounds later from the lips of the Baptist (John 3.11-18, 3.31-36). From a deeper point of view, the source of the Baptist's teaching is the Logos. For the Baptist knows about the one who is to come, the *Erchoménos* (John 15.17 and 30; Matt. 11.3; Luke 7.19; John 3.31; 6.14; 11.27; Rev. 1.8), whom the Prologue already named as the true light (John 1.9). Through the *Erchoménos*, the kingdom of heaven is at hand. But the Baptist also knows who is the *First*. The *Erchoménos*, the spirit-being, who in the end enters a human body as the last,[17] is the First (*prótos*), the firstborn of creation. As it says in Revelations, "I am Alpha and Omega, the first and the last, the beginning and the end" (Rev. 1.8; 21.6. See also 1.11.),[18] the beginning of creation (*arché*) (Rev. 3.14; Col. 1.15). What the Baptist knew of the First is concealed by the translation. This reads: "This was he of whom I spake, he that cometh after me is preferred before me: for he was before me" (John 1.15). "After me cometh a man which is preferred before me: for he was before me" (John 1.30). The translation of the passage "is preferred before me" in the King James Version of the Gospel does not quite convey the real meaning. Nor does Luther's German version,

"... who has been before me, for he was earlier than I," make sense, since it merely repeats the same thing in different ways. Besides, Jesus of Nazareth was born a little later than John the Baptist. The correct translation is: "The *Erchoménos*, coming after me has become (*gégonen*) greater, more powerful than I, because he was (*én*) the First before me." *Gégonen* and *én* — *has, become* and *was* — are placed very consciously, because the First (*Prótos*), the first and not before, was always before me. This means: He who comes later than I, has become greater than I, for he was the First of my kind, i.e. the Logos-being. In the synoptic Gospels (Matt. 3.11; Mark 1.7; Luke 3.16) we read "mightier than I." The key verbs of the Prologue — "was" and "has become" — are used in a coherent fashion here too. As an earthly being, the Logos-being "has become" one who has "gone beyond" the Baptist, for he *was* the first of his kind from all eternity. Knowledge of the *Prótos*, the *Erchoménos*, is the older form of knowledge concerning the one who later and more precisely was called "Logos."

But the Baptist is also aware of the *end*, of the wrath of God and of the final "*Ekpýrosis*,"[19] the consequence of God's wrath (Matt. 3.7 and 11; Luke 3.7 and 17). God's wrath abides on those who do not allow themselves to be convinced by the Son (John 3.36).

Whoever does not cognize the Logos within the being of God meets with God's wrath. Therefore Moses is denied entry to the promised land. When he searches a second time for water out of the rock, instead of "speaking" to it, as God had commanded him to do, he strikes the rock twice with his staff (Deut. 20.8-13; Numbers 3.26; 4.21). Thus he does not recognize the Logos behind the figure of Jehovah. Moses's difficulties in speaking are recorded (Exodus 4.10-15; 6.29-7.1). The opposite of "wrath" is "eternal life"(1.John 5.12), which still remains to be discussed.

The Old Testament stands almost entirely under the sign of wrath. The law guides events toward the birth of Jesus, and behind the law stands the idea of the Logos, the invisible God. Thus transgression of the law—because the Logos was not understood—is followed by God's wrath.

The positive aspect of the epoch of the law is the possibility of becoming a child of God, i.e. of being able to act out of the divine principle working in man. This relationship to God is different from the Son's relationship to God. The Son is—as we have already shown—of the same essence as the Father; they are one (John 10.30; 17.11 and 22). Old Testament man, even Moses, cannot look upon the face of God.[20] The fact that Moses was expected to cognize the potential of the *magic word* shows how high he stood above his contemporaries, even if he failed at the task. To see God's face and to live was not granted him (Exodus 33.20-23). Even though his "obituary" reports that he saw God face to face, this contradicts the scriptural evidence. Moses has to cover his face, when he comes near to God (Exodus 3.6). On the other hand, having been with God, Moses had to veil his shining face so that those about him would not fear him (Exodus 34.29-35).

This inability to see God's countenance corresponds to his wrath. This is clearly quite different from the prophecy, "And they shall see his face" (Rev. 22.4). St. Paul and St. John confirm this prophecy (2.Cor. 3.7-18; 1.Cor. 13.12; 1.John 3.2). God's countenance, however, is the Son, the

Logos, who had to give up his divinity to a large degree, so that men might endure him.

The Baptist knows that he who comes after him is the Son. His words echo what the Logos earlier said about himself (John 3.11-19).

He also knows the cosmic background of the one who is to come: that he is the *Lamb of God* (John 1.29 and 36). This theme appears only in St. John's Gospel. "Lamb of God" was the name given to the cosmic being who had the task of self-sacrifice. Creation — evolution — consists in the continuous detaching of creatures from their origin, of their withdrawal and alienation. This is necessary, but it is a "sin" if the "separation" is not accompanied by a consciousness of the primal union and a knowledge of the origin, the primal self. At first, however, this is impossible. Man must leave; he must lose and forget his origin. The origin must become *hidden* from him. These "negative" movements of detachment and alienation are contained esoterically in the Greek verb *lanthánein*, which means to forget, to lose, to hide. It is the root of the noun *léthe*, and this in turn gives rise to the word for "truth." *Alétheia*, truthfulness, means unhiddenness, not-forgetting, not-losing. The Lamb is the being who takes on himself the "sins" connected with creation in this sense. The Lamb sacrifices himself for these sins. Thereby he brings *alétheia* (John 1.14 and 17) and takes on the destiny of man in the ultimate sense. And by that he bears witness in the world of men to the origin, the Father.

Through baptism by water man consciously experienced — in the body — what in an earlier phase of its cosmic history humanity lived through in a dream-like consciousness, without conscious experience. John the Baptist points at him who baptizes with fire and with the spirit, who addresses himself to the purely spiritual in man (Matt. 3.11; Mark 1.8; Luke 3.16; John 1.27 and 33). Everywhere the text speaks of baptizing "with the holy spirit and with fire." This "baptism," literally a cleansing, is distinguished from all earlier procedures in that it takes place without the use of any outer element, such as water, or any outer means. It occurs within the human spirit. This change in the spirit is so powerful that its effects reach right into the blood and warmth of man.[21] Indeed, the spirit works right into the human warmth-organization: cognition transforms man through and through, even to his very blood. This hints at a distant possibility which is very important for the fate of humanity. Today the ecology of human warmth is largely maintained by processes of combustion, made possible through inhaled oxygen. It is well known that in the plant, apart from the processes of combustion through sunlight, there are also opposite reductive processes at work, through which new combustibles are created out of water and carbon dioxide, themselves the products of combustion. In this way oxygen is liberated. For millenia it was known that man would one day be able to nourish himself like a plant. But for that he cannot use the sun's external rays since he lacks the chlorophyll which arises in the plant by means of the sun's rays, and which makes the sun's forces available for the nourishment of the plant. An *inner sun* must light up, to allow for a corresponding process to occur in man.

"He must increase, but I must decrease" (John 3.30), says the one of whom it is written: "He was not the light, but came to bear witness of the light." The verb "increase" here means the same as it meant in Heraclitus's sentence: "The soul has a Logos within it, which increases out of itself." The ego-being, the self-constituted individual, who needs what is "outer," the outer light, in order to experience himself through the light, must decrease, in order that the true I, the source of light, may begin to shine in man. But also, the whole of the old world, the old knowledge, must fade away for the *true light* (John 1.9) to enter the world. This is the light that bears witness of itself. Because it is true (*alethinón*), it transilluminates itself. In a certain sense this light was already in the world; but the world could not know this, because "self-constituted," individualized human beings had not yet taken hold of it. Now, for the third time, it seeks to enter the world in a new way. First it came through creation, which was made entirely by the Logos (John 1.3); then it came to the "children of God"; and now it seeks to enter the world in such a way that it will be recognized as "the world," as reality, as the fundamental reality of which the world consists. For this to happen, the true light had to enter man, so that he could recognize the light-nature of the world as the radiance, the glory of the only begotten Son.

The true light can bear witness of itself. No one else could bear witness of this light. For, to do so, he would have to use this very same light as a witness.

Two verses in Chapters 5 and 8 describe the stages of the process by which the being of the Logos enters the human being. In Chapter 5 the Lord does not bear witness of himself: "If I bear witness of myself, my witness is not true" (John 5.31). He refers to other witnesses (John 3.33), to his deeds and to his Father (John 5.36,37), and to Moses (John 5.46). Then, in Chapter 8, he says: "Though I bear witness of myself, yet my witness is true [*alethés*]" (John 8.14). What happened between these two statements? In Chapter 6, the feeding of the five thousand is described. The true (*alethinón*) bread from heaven is spoken of (John 6.32). Jesus says "I am the bread of life" (John 6.35,48,51). His flesh and blood are the true (*alethés*) bread and the true drink (John 6.55). In Chapter 7, Jesus speaks about the living water, which shall flow out of the belly of him to whom he gives to drink, and who believes in him (John 7.37,38). The text here refers to the Holy Spirit. Whoever receives the Spirit becomes its source. Chapter 8 begins with the adulteress, whose sin Jesus writes on the ground and who, contrary to the law, is not stoned to death. For none of those who accuse her feels free of sin. The epoch of the law is over. After this scene the sentence rings out: "I am the light of the world: he that followeth me shall not walk in darkness, but shall have the light of life" (John 8.12). And, following this quotation, he gives the Pharisees the "reason": "For I know whence I came, and whither I go" (John 8.14). Earlier, the same is said of the wind, the spirit (John 3.8).

The narrative in these chapters elaborates what was earlier summed up in the Prologue: the true (*alethinón*) light was coming. The true bread and drink, and even, by way of anticipation, the spirit of truth, *alétheia*, are spoken of in the I AM form (John 14.17; 15.26; 16.13), leading up to the greatest of the I AM sayings: "I am the light of the world."

In the background of human consciousness lies the primal experience which cannot be expressed in words but only thought: "I am" and "light." The tiniest movement of consciousness is accompanied by this hidden experience; indeed any movement can only occur under this "condition." In everyday consciousness this primal experience is always concealed by the experience of the "that." The eye only looks. Following the logic of the Logos, it may be understood that "that" can only exist for *me*, for an I, and this only through cognition, through light. But only very seldom, and in a heightened state of consciousness, can this become experience. Not experiencing this results in the naiveté of contemporary man, i.e. in the superstition of a reality which is assumed to have an existence independent of cognition, and which includes neither the knowing subject nor the process of cognition. That man today can *speak* about this problem, even if only in a negative sense, shows that he has the possibility and the capacity to approach what has always been the essence of every authentic teaching. The fact that in earlier times this could not be experienced may be called "the state of forgetting or losing." For modern man, however, we would have to call it "to sin against the Holy Spirit." But since it is the Spirit itself that enables man to deny the Spirit — out of naiveté, as shown above — this sin can be redeemed by man alone. Spirit is now man's own spirit: no forgiveness of this sin can come from without.

Even without this primal experience, consciousness may speak about the light, but this light is not the true, self-transilluminating light, which does not forget and lose itself. The light that ordinary consciousness may speak of is not the unconcealed light of "*alétheia*," not the light of the Word, the Logos.

The reality of the primal experience — "I am," "light" — is the root of consciousness. This was "taught," in some form or other, in all times. Before Christianity it was done without words, through a vision — in a supersensible, i.e. intuitive state of consciousness — of that being who can say: "(the) I am (is) the light of the world." The vision was the teaching. But this vision also meant that the being saw those who beheld it: there was only *one* seeing. This experience was not earthly; it was not made in this world. Now, however, the *true* light wants to come *into* the world, wants to become part of the world as we understand it today. It wants to become reality for mankind. If human beings recognize it in this new and unaccustomed garment, then it enters the human body. It becomes visible to the eye, and touchable by the hand (1.John 1.1). The primal mystery which was hidden throughout eternity comes into the open, into *alétheia*. "Blessed are the eyes which see the things that ye see: For I tell you, that many prophets and kings have desired to see those things which ye see, and have not seen them" (Luke 10.23-24; Matt. 13.16). The true Light now stands before men in earthly visibility. Are men blessed? No, because they do not see him. Their pre-conceptions of the Messiah conceal him. The Evangelist has to emphasize explicitly that Jesus was the Christ (1.John 1.1; 2.2; 4.2). John is perhaps the only one who already understood this before the resurrection.

The Son is the Father's consciousness. No man comes to the Father but through the Son (Matt. 11.27; Luke 10.22). The Son is the Father's consciousness, even in man. "His —the Father's—Logos does not abide in you: you do not recognize the Son" (John 5.38).

The primal experience is put into words by the Evangelist. This is a great step compared to the "mute" experiences of the spirit in earlier times. The primal experience is now made accessible to every human being who can *live* with these words. A new experience blossoms out of them. One may call it "the light of the word." Man awakens in the word. The awakening brings him a new ability: to bear witness, as his prototype does, to what he bears within himself. The Son becomes "the faithful and true (*alethinós*) witness" (Rev. 3.14). "He that believeth on the Son of God hath the witness in himself" (1.John 5.10). "He that hath the Son hath life; and he that hath not the Son of God hath no life" (1.John 5.12).

The Logos bears witness of itself. It counts itself as one of the two necessary witnesses (John 8.17-18). The other witness is the Father (John 5.37; 8.18). In the future, the Spirit will be the witness (John 15.26; 14.26), but for now, St. John the Evangelist testifies. He sums up the whole theme of "witnessing." "This is he that came by water and blood, even Jesus Christ; not by water only, but by water and blood. And it is the Spirit that beareth witness, because the Spirit is truth. For there are three that bear record in heaven, the Father, the Word, and the Holy Ghost: and these three are one. And there are three that bear witness in earth, the Spirit, and the water, and the blood: and these three agree in one" (1.John 5.6-8).

The Logos speaks through a human body and a human soul. These tools must adapt themselves gradually to the spirit, whose bearer they are. From Chapter 5 onwards one can follow the stages of this growth of consciousness. The feeding of the five thousand: "My body, my blood, are bread and drink, the *true* nourishment and the true drink." Whoever believes in him becomes a spring of living water. The speaker grows one with the earth, becomes the new spirit of the earth[22] — *my* body, *my* blood — but he is at the same time the one who says this of himself, who bears witness and who is therefore the *true* bread and the *true* drink (*alethés*). The miraculous filling of so many people sitting on the earth — it is emphasized that "there was *much grass* in the place" (John 6.10; Matt. 14.19; Mark 6.39) — already stands under this sign of earthly growth, likewise the awakening of Lazarus, who is laid in the earth. These stages are followed by the sayings about the light of the world, expressed in inadequate earthly pictures (John 8.12; 9.5; 11.9-10; 12.35-36, 46). The Light-God, the Sun-God, awakens in the human body. The one who was born blind is healed. The "I am," the light of the world, continually expands: "I am the door" (John 10.9); "the good shepherd" (John 10.11-14); "I and the Father are one" (John 10.30); "I am the resurrection and the life" (John 11.25); "I am the way, the truth, and the life" (John 14.6); "I am the true vine" (John 15.1). But all these are only variations on the theme: "I am the light of the world." This phrase inaugurates the overcoming of dualism, of light and darkness, of dualistic cognition. The new wisdom begins: light in light. "This then is the message which we have heard of him, and declare unto you, that God is light, and in him is no darkness at all" (1.John 1.5). "Again a new commandment I write unto you, which is true in him and in you: because the darkness disappears and the true light now shineth" (1.John 2.8). It is stressed: the *true* light, not the light which shines in the darkness.

The one who overcomes duality is the "only-begotten," *monógenes* (John 1.14,18; 3.16). *Monógenes* means, the son has not two parents, but is born of One: nothing else intervenes, for everything else became through him. Everything else, every other concept, is doubly begotten. The *Monógenes* is not *a* word, not this or that, but *the* word, the Word speaking itself, the I-Am-here: the Father's consciousness, the substance of the primal experience.

Chapter 11 divides even the form of the Gospel into two parts. Through the raising of Lazarus, the beloved disciple *becomes*. He is "that disciple" or "the other disciple" (John

13.23; 18.15-16; 19.26-27, 35; 20.2-4,8; 20.21,24),[23] the third witness. Just before the raising of Lazarus, the text returns for the last time to the Baptist (John 10.40-41), in order, as it were, to stay, to abide near him (John 10.40), and thereby to grow for the next deed. The raising of Lazarus occurs through the earth, whose spirit the Logos has become, and within which the "infirm" body lies. This deed, the last of the miracles and signs (John 11.47), becomes the cause of the final conflict with the high priests and Pharisees (John 11.47-53) and is the reason for the crucifixion. Following this, the Baptist is no longer mentioned. The Logos speaks and reveals itself (John 12.17), ending in the great "I-am" phrase (John 18.5), after which those who try to arrest him fall to the ground. Then he departs from the world into which he came, and the beloved disciple, John, bears witness of both the departed and the resurrected one. Just so the Baptist bore witness to the *Erchoménos*, the one who was to come. The Evangelist's testimony is called "true" — *alethiné, alethés*: "And he who saw it bare witness and his witness is true; and he knows that he speaks true, that you might believe" (John 19.35). "This is the disciple who testifies of these things and wrote these things; and we know that his testimony is true" (John 21.24). We find the same in the Epistle of John (1.John 5.10), while, in Revelation, he became a "true witness," like the Logos itself (Rev. 3.14).

Those who were able to bear witness of the Logos were called "servants of the Logos, as it was from the beginning." This refers to knowledge of the beginning, in which the Logos was, of the beginning, which was the Logos. The expression "servant of the word" does not appear in John's Gospel, but is found in Luke: ". . . as they delivered unto us, who from the beginning were eye-witnesses and ministers of the word..." (Luke 1.2). The phrase "from the beginning," *ap'archés*, appears several times in this context (John 15.27; 1.John 1.1; 2.13-14,24; 3.11). According to the text, however, there can be no doubt that the fourth Evangelist himself "became" a servant of the Logos.

John the Baptist was not a servant of the Logos. "He will be lesser than the least in the kingdom of heaven, which is within you." The Baptist was not baptized with fire and the spirit. He testified to the truth, but not as a "true witness" who carries the evidence of the truth in himself. He does not "tarry" as the "other disciple" does (John 21.22-23). He is the greatest among those who recognize the Logos, but he does not participate in the great metamorphosis of the spirit of the earth which is called into life by the incarnation. Nevertheless, there is a mysterious and manifold relationship between the two Johns.

FIVE

The Speaker

> We say purity, we say rose,
> we resemble all that happens;
> but behind it lies the nameless,
> our true form and place.
> *Rilke*

The possibility of directing humanity's attention to the Logos alters with the change of human consciousness. This change occurs in response to appropriate changes in schooling—in each case the Logos is beheld in a form corresponding to the change.

In earlier times, wordless methods prevail. No expression exists for the light of the word, which works from within and from without at the same time. The true light is not yet perceived. Heraclitus therefore begins his book with the sentence: "Even though this Logos is always. . . ." This sentence—especially the word "this"—was, and still is, a great riddle for philologists, because it indicates something as familiar which has not yet been discussed. After all, we are dealing with the very first sentence of the book. Wilhelm Kelber tries to solve this problem in his excellent study[24] by pointing out that Heraclitus offered his book at the feet of the statue of Artemis at Ephesus, or at least in her temple,

THE SPEAKER

which is that of the pre-Christian Logos-mysteries.[25] From this point of view, therefore, the word "this" would refer to the first *thought* of the Logos as this was *experienced* in the mysteries. Although this solution seems to make sense, it is probably too modern: it presupposes a consciousness that can mentally understand all these relations. We find similar structures in Zen Buddhist stories. Here the student's questions are met by the master's apparently irrelevant answers and sometimes even with blows—either of which is intended to draw attention away from the content of the discourse and to focus instead on the speaking, the dialogue as such, the happening between I and you. In a wider sense even a blow is a sign, meaning: I have heard you, and you hear me. Sometimes, the dialogue is suddenly interrupted by the question: What is that? Even though Zen Buddhism is active today, it is nevertheless pre-Christian in its attitude towards consciousness. Its central intention is to point to the word, not by teaching in words, but by realizing the presence of the word between human beings, and by directing the attention to the still living, floating word. The same explanation seems to hold for Heraclitus' "this" which draws the attention directly to the Logos. Confronting the reader in the first sentence as "this" Logos, it points to the *actual*, present word, the Logos, which makes possible communication between the writer and the reader of Heraclitus' book.

If one may call such indications and instructions "indirect," then one finds in St. John's Gospel a much more direct pedagogical method for turning the inner gaze to the word, and through the word, to the speaker, the one capable of words. Even though the Logos is described in the Prologue as a divine *person*, it could also be explained as an abstract principle, as, indeed, many interpreters of the text

59

BECOMING AWARE OF THE LOGOS

have done. But many turns of phrase and formulations contradict this. They show that we are dealing with the spoken word and with the principle which makes men capable of speech.

For instance, a phrase which appears more than twenty times in St. John's Gospel is: "Amen, amen, I say unto you..." To be sure, we also find a similar formula, with a single "Amen," in other Gospels, but not as frequently nor as emphatically as in St. John. "Amen" is not "Verily," as Luther and others have translated it. *Amen* is name, the name of a being. "Amen, Amen, I say unto you," really means: "I, Amen, say unto you." In this way "Amen" is used as name in the Apocalypse (Rev. 3.14). Amen means: "So be it." As a name, this word means a being, who is already so, for whom it is already *so*; a being, whom human beings call upon in order that, as it is unto him, it might be so with them too, that they also might be so, like him. (1.John 3.2). This being speaks to men in the figure of Jesus, emphasizing that he *speaks*, that he is the speaking-being of the world. It is actually superfluous to say: "I say unto you...," for what is said proves that it has been said. The emphasis "I say..." shifts the attention away from a one-sided understanding of the content to the *saying* itself, to the speaker. It points to the fact that what is spoken is *spoken*, that something passes from the speaker to the hearer.

Clearly the same theme is dealt with when Christ raises from the dead the widow's son of Nain (Luke 7.14) and Jairus' daughter (Mark 5.41). The Logos-bearer says: "Young man (or damsel) *I say to you*, arise." Both here and in the "Amen, Amen..." phrases, the Greek word is "*légo*." This indicates a very conscious, indeed earthly-conscious kind of speech. I know that I am saying something. This means

60

that in these cases it is the earthly I-forces that are being addressed. The I is being asked to reunite with the earthly body after its connection with the body has been loosened or separated. The human consciousness is supposed to notice this speaking, which is conscious of itself, and of which the speaker himself is aware during the act of speaking: "Amen, Amen, I say unto you." For contemporary man, such reflection on one's own actions is, in principle and with good will, not difficult. However, he is inclined to forget his present activity, so that the reflection, if it occurs at all, remains an abstract, *posterior* examination of what he did. The average man of 2,000 years ago was still quite unaccustomed to this gesture of consciousness: the Ram's backward gaze. In two other cases (Mark 9.27 and Matt. 8.15) only the corresponding pointing gesture is mentioned,[26] similarly as when in the above quoted passages he touches with his hand Jarius' daughter and the coffin of the young man of Nain. At the raising of Lazarus neither speech nor gesture are mentioned; instead there is reference to a cry: "Lazarus, come forth!" In this case we are dealing with an entirely different event.

When the Logos-bearer reveals himself, he uses a unique formula. He says to the Samaritan woman: "If thou knewest the gift of God, and who it is that saith (*légon*) to thee: Give me to drink, thou would have asked of him . . ." (John 4.10). Later, when the woman speaks about the coming of the Messiah, the Logos-bearer says: "I am (the one), who is speaking to you" (John 4.26). These words are repeated in almost identical fashion in the conversation with the man born blind, who was healed by the Logos-bearer, and whom the Pharisees expelled from the community. He asks about the Son of God, that he may pray to him: "Jesus said to him: you have seen him, and the one speaking to you is he"

(John 9.37). In these two sentences "the one speaking" — the speaker — is expressed not by the verb *légo*, but by "*lalô, hó lálon.*" The word "*lalo, laléo*" means, on the one hand "to lull, to babble childishly" and, on the other hand, super-earthly speech, i.e., to announce, to prophesy." It is used very consistently, not for everyday, earthly-conscious, or reflective speech, but for inspired speech that communicates directly out of the spirit. Likewise it is used by St. Paul (1.Cor. 13; 1.Cor. 14) for "speaking in tongues," "speaking by the spirit of God" (1.Cor. 12.3), and elsewhere for prophetic, Pentecostal, and angelic speaking (Luke 24.25,44; Acts 2.4-6; Rev. 21.9) etc. In St. John's Gospel, this word *lalo*, is clearly used for "revelatory" speech — that is, for accounts of the supersensible. In these instances it should really say: "I am the revealer." We have to understand it in this way when the servants of the Pharisees say: "Never a man spake (*lalo*), like this man spake" (John 7.46). What the servants say is emphasized by the repetition of the words "man" and "spake" and expresses at the same time their doubt, "Is he a man? Is he really . . . ?", which they do not want to express openly. Yet the Pharisees discover nevertheless that their servants have been convinced (John 7.47-48), at which Nicodemus stands up, who also privately is convinced that He is the Messiah.

But the sentences by which the Logos-being reveals himself are not logical in an earthly sense. It sufficed to say: I am (he), because it is self-evident that he is the speaker and the revealer. The emphasis on "the speaker" here indicates a special theme. Who is the speaker? He is the one in man, whom one does not usually see and recognize. What we see of man is outer appearance, the speaker is mediator, not the speaker himself. The speaker is pure presence, in every sense.

62

THE SPEAKER

If I speak to someone, I and he must be *there*, must be present. Everyday consciousness however is a consciousness[27] of the past, without the experience of the present. This consciousness of the past only knows those contents that have already been thought, already been perceived, already been represented. Therefore, to focus on the speaker has two goals. *The true subject* must be perceived; but we must also perceive that this subject does not appear without mediation. In order to cognize the speaker, consciousness must be raised into the present. This means, in the language of the Gospel, it must be lifted into *life*. In the case of the one who was born blind, the difference between the past and the present is emphasized: "You have both seen him — the Son of God, for whom the healed one asks — and it is he who is talking with you" (John 9.37). When has the one healed seen him? At the very moment they are talking he stands before him. But, seeing him, the blind man can barely recognize his presence. Yet, in "the speaker," whom he divines behind the visible figure, he can feel the one who is present: the one who opened his eyes.

A fourth instance of this occurs in Chapter 8 (John 8.25). This describes the inner struggle to cognize the Logos in human form. Only in this way does a person become truly human. This is "the third birth," by which a man gives birth to himself. Whoever does not achieve this, dies in his sins, forgetting his origin, and not attaining to presence, to life. "You are from below, I am from above; you are of this world, I am not of this world. I said therefore to you, that you shall die in your sins, for if you believe not that I am, you shall die in your sins. Then they said to him: Who are you? (John 8.23-25). Jesus answered them: Firstly, I am who I announce to you; I am who I announce to you from the beginning; I am the one who announces the beginning to you. The revealer, the being who reveals itself in man through speaking, is the I-am-here: "here" in the sense of presence. This is also his name: I-am-here. The I lives in whoever can say I am. The ability to say I am, shows that man can realize his divinity, for God himself calls himself by this name. But everyday man misuses this name. He never uses it in such a way that he really refers to *himself*, and not to something else, which is not *I*, something that is, for example, *mine*: my body, my soul, even *my* I.[28]

If the I am is spoken of in the true sense, it means the one who is present, who does not need to rely on *anything*, on an object, on the past. Ordinary consciousness cannot exist without feeling itself through something opposed to it, which is past, from which it can distinguish itself. In this distinction it feels and experiences itself, and this distinction is at the same time the gesture by which the present is turned into the past, life is killed, and the brother becomes an opponent. This is the gesture of Cain. Without it there would be no consciousness, no cognition to begin with. The Christian impulse means that the necessity of this gesture is overcome and that through this overcoming a true I is born. The gesture of Cain is the original "sin," the root and origin of all other sins.

The I am phrase is used in the Greek text of the Gospel in a way that is difficult to render in many languages. In Greek, the question: "Is it you?" is not answered by "*It* is I," but only by "I am." This is the form it takes in, for instance, John 4.26 and John 9.37. One could well ask, therefore, regarding the translation, whether the added "he" —"I am *he*"—does not conceal the meaning. The word "I am," however, is clearly used as a name: "If you do not

64

believe that I am, you will die in your sins" (John 8.24). Usually, "that I am" is translated by "that I am *he*," which is meaningless because it is not evident to whom or what the "he" refers. The I am by itself is also used by John: "Before Abraham was, I am" (John 8.28,58). In all these places one could say, for instance, although ungrammatically, "If you do not believe in the I am . . ." or "Before Abraham became, the I am exists." In a similar form the I am arises in the one born blind: "Some said: this is he; others said: he is like him; but he said: I am he." In Greek, "he said that I am" (John 9.9). Here the little Greek word *autós* would be appropriate, corresponding to the English "It is I" as in Luke 24.39: "Behold my hands and my feet, that it is I myself, *hotí egó eimí autós*. St. John certainly uses the I am in the true sense, when he writes: "Now I tell you before it come, that, when it is come to pass, you may believe that I am" (John 13,19). Here the translation reads "that I am he," but again one does not know to whom the "he" refers.

The power of the word becomes clear in the scene of the arrest (John 18.5-6). When the "band" and the servants say they are seeking Jesus of Nazareth, Jesus says to them, "I am (he)": "And Judas also, which betrayed him, stood with them. As soon then as he had said unto them, I am, they went backward, and fell to the ground." Here too, the word which would correspond to *it* or *he* is missing in the Greek text. The interpolated remark about Judas indicates that he also "went backward and fell to the ground."

That the I am is not used in an ordinary sense is proven by the last sentence of St. Matthew's Gospel: "And lo, I am with you all the days even unto the end of the aeon" (Matt. 28.20). Here "*egó eimí*," I am, is used, instead of the future form: I will be with you. Again, if one looks at John 8.58,

"Before Abraham has become, I am," one can see that this I am phrase cannot be used in either past or future tense, for this unique noun form combines and bridges past, present and future.²⁹

As he already revealed himself in the figure of Jehovah, the name of the Logos is I-am-here. But when his name is under consideration as for instance in "... those who believed in his name" (John 1.9), we may ask: What is meant by this allusion to the name? What is meant by the emphasis on believing in his name or in himself? What does the name mean in relation to the being, whose name it is?

Ferdinand Ebner³⁰ interprets the phrase "to believe in the name of God" in the following way: "To believe in the name of God means to believe in God as the invoked being, as the "addressed person" as the thou corresponding to man's I — in other words, to believe in God's personal existence. But the phrase "to believe in the *name* of God" also emphasizes the connection of faith with the word. And, truly, all faith is faith in the "word" in the final and deepest sense."

This is doubtless a very meaningful interpretation, but, again, perhaps too "modern," in the sense that only through a development directed at just this possibility is it possible to see the name, the word. In earlier times name and being were united. This is no longer the case. An emphasis on the name was always a part of the schooling that introduced today's state of consciousness — a consciousness capable of distinguishing between name and being — thereby making nominalism possible. The true name is more than the name assigned in any given language. The ability to make this distinction belongs to our potential self-consciousness, our potentially word-less thinking. This arose *through* word-thinking and is a step towards overcoming what the Bible

66

calls the Tower of Babel. It is a step towards a universal human language, the language of thinking which, identical behind all languages, represents a remnant of the primal language. The nominalists did not realize that even their own theory presupposed a primal language. The collective concepts, which they regarded as "mere" names, presupposed wordless, "nameless" concepts.[31]

This relationship between being and name also lives, on a cosmic scale, in the relation between the Father and the Son. For the Son *is the name* of the Father. To the signs of countenance and hand is now added this third sign, which appears only in consciousness. For man to perceive the name of God, the *one* and *invisible* God, to receive, comprehend and grasp his name, he must be able to say *I* to himself in the true sense. This is what it means to pray "in his name," "in the name of the I-am-here," to believe in the I-am-here. This is the only name of God which is really eternal, I-am-here (Exodus 3.15); Isa. 42.8): in Greek: *egó eimí.* This name is a world-principle which appears first to Moses, then in the Psalms and to the Prophets, and finally—that the times might be fullfilled—appears in this world, in earthly visibility, so that all men may be able to receive it. Yet comprehending, understanding, receiving are still soul-gestures of the individual human being, which corresponds to the fact that the divine could once be experienced only by the individual, through initiation in the mysteries. The passages in the Prologue and elsewhere about "receiving" must be understood in this sense (John 1.5,11-12; 5.43). God let his son come down to the earth. He is the *Erchoménos*, the appearance or name of God, by which he reveals himself and by which he can be invoked—the Son is all this. This is how we must understand the following passages: "I and my

Father are one" (John 10.30); "the Father is in me and I in him" (John 10.38); "He that honoureth not the Son honoreth not the Father" (John 5.23); "For I am not alone, but I and the Father that sent me" (John 8.16); "If you had known me, you should have known my Father also" (John 8.19); "And he that seeth me seeth him that sent me" (John 12.45); "No man cometh to the Father but by me" (John 14.6); "he that hath seen me hath seen the Father" (John 14.9); "but the Father that dwelleth in me, he doeth the works" (John 14.10); (likewise John 14.11,13,20; 15.23; 16.5; 17.6,11,21; Matt. 11.27; Luke 10.22).

The Son is the Father's word, his name. His name is: I-am-here. This is the name of the Word, of the Logos, and of the Father too. For the name is like the being whose name it is. "And his name is called the Word of God" as it is quite literally translated (Rev. 19.13). What is his name like? It is like him. We are facing the open secret of the Word, the Son, the Father: of Man. This then is also how we must understand the following: "... and I will write upon him the name of my God, and the name of the city of my God, which is new Jerusalem, which cometh down out of heaven from my God: and I will write upon him my new name" (Rev. 3.12). It is all the same name. "He that believeth on him is not condemned: but he that believeth not is condemned already, because he hath not believed in the name of the only begotten Son of God" (Rev. 22.4; John 3.18); "I am come in my father's name, and you receive me not. If another shall come in the name of his individual being,[32] him you will receive" (John 5.43); "But these are written, that you might believe that Jesus is the Christ, the Son of God; and that believing you might have life in his name" (John 20.31).

THE SPEAKER

The Son appears on earth. He does not appear in order to be worshipped later, in memory, as God's son. When his appearance disappears from humanity — at the Ascension — his force can still arise, first in the disciples, and later in more and more people: "Amen, Amen, I say unto you, he that believeth on me, the works that I do shall he do also; and greater works than these shall he do" (John 14.12). The unnameable name is named. The never seen face of God reveals itself to all men — a new earth, a new heaven.

But humanity so far has hardly understood this cosmic-earthly event. That the relation of the Son to the Father was not understood, made possible nominalism with all its consequences. The entire anti-Christian age in which we live comes out of this. In this age the work of John may be a guide to make amends for it.

SIX

Life

> Of all greatly dared existences
> Can any be braver and more glowing?
> We stand and brace ourselves
> against our boundaries
> and draw something indiscernible within.
> *Rilke*

Dying "in your sins"; the wrath of God, which abides on one who does not believe in the Son; the absence of the Logos, its not in-dwelling or abiding in man, not to love the Logos (John 8.42) — such is the everyday-consciousness of humanity to whom the Logos appeared.

Out of these negative features a *world* forms. In St. John's Gospel it is called "this world." "This world" is the world of past-consciousness, the dualistic world, which has no present and no real future, but only a future which is calculable and hence already past, abstractly represented, "non-existent." Often, in the text, it is simply called "world" (John 17, several times). Neither the Logos nor his kingdom is of this world (John 8.23, 18.36). There is a prince of this world (John 12.31; 16.11; Eph. 2.2), who has no share in the Logos-bearer (John 14.30) and who was overcome and cast out by him (John 12.13). Victory over this world (John

16.33; 1.John 4.4; 5.4) — its overcoming — means that the world is no longer experienced in its past, in its standing-over-against, but is experienced in its full reality — an experience called "life," in contrast to the world of death. Whoever "conquers," participates in this life, passes over from death into life (John 3.14).

Everyday-consciousness does not know what life is. It neither has an adequate concept of life, nor can it perceive it. One cannot distinguish by perception between a dead seed and a living one. It is characteristic of everyday-consciousness that in order to exist at all it needs both the past and the inside-outside. It does not know life, for life is the present. Thus consciousness faces a world which, because it is made up of the past, actually represents a diminished reality, because reality cannot be the past. Therefore we are brought to conclude that the true reality of the world is what we call life — without knowing what life is. Initially everyday-consciousness needs the world of the past, inner and outer. Separated from "this world," its opposite, it becomes self-consciousness. This explains the action of Cain: what is dead always arises from what is living, not from itself. Self-consciousness can begin to work to overcome this action, to become "victorious" over "this world." In today's human consciousness self-consciousness is a "subject" in the "present." It looks upon the past, upon what has been thought and perceived and, in this activity, experiences itself in a dreamlike manner. To look upon the past without awareness is the gesture of the Ram, but it is distorted, misused, uncompleted. Through it, "this world" comes into being in the constellation of the double death of man and of the world. The human task is to experience this gesture of the Ram consciously. Without awareness, it is sickness, sin, death. The Lamb can redeem this sin. Today this entrance into life (1.John 3.14; John 5.24) can occur with the aid of exercises in consciousness. In St. John's time, however, the way to life was faith in the I-am-here, in his name, in the Son. Believing was the way for *all* men, for, in principle, everybody has the ability to believe. Such faith is not belief in the contemporary sense—"I believe, because I cannot know"—but is an inner conviction, which may be compared with the contemporary experience of evidence, for example, in mathematics, but which has a much broader scope. It is the certitude of the religious: *it is so*. For St. John's time, faith was in every way a cognitive experience, not a substitute for cognition.

Another world stands over against wrath, death and sin: the world of life, of "*alétheia*," the consciousness that does not submerge itself in "*léthe*," and therefore knows neither death, nor extinction of consciousness. This life is not a biological concept. Biological life is not "lived," which means that it does not occur consciously, is not "experienced." Insofar as the concept and the percept of a thing together constitute a "reality," we do not "have" life for we have neither its percept nor its concept. The life meant here is a living reality, neither outside nor inside. It means that man experiences the presence of the processes of consciousness and does not sleep through them. Thereby a living world is revealed to him, which is more real than past-consciousness. Wilhelm Kelber puts this most beautifully: "Where thinking grasps life, it is also grasped by life."[33] The life of thinking, living thinking, and the life of the world are one *experience*: victory. This victory is also mentioned in the Apocalypse with respect to the seven communities (Rev. 2.7, 11, 17, 26; 3.5, 12, 21). The victor is promised life, to him it will be granted to eat of the tree of life. He shall not be hurt by the second death; he will be given some of the hidden manna and a white stone with a new name written on it which no one knows except the one who receives it; he will be given power over the nations; he shall be clad in white garments and his name will not be blotted out of the book of life; he will become a pillar in the temple of God, and upon him the name of God, and of the new Jerusalem and the Son's new name will be written; and he will sit with the Son on his throne.

The world of life knows neither time in the earthly sense, nor space.[34] It is the lowest heaven. The creative beings, the hierarchies, therefore, know neither time nor space, but, like the world of life, like truth (*alétheia*), are timeless and spaceless. Thus they could not create space and time — a world of the past — for man. Yet it was just this world that man needed. For this to happen, a being had to be allowed to enter into the world — a being who had his existence only in "this world" — the prince of this world, who could create the dead, the life-less, the kingdom of the past which is foreign to the gods. This kingdom is not entirely without light and life. If it were, it would be without qualities, which is to say, it would not exist for man — even though science seeks for a particle without quality, out of which to build up a qualitative world.[35] The true life contains the light of men (John 1.5). It is a light-filled life in the Logos. For man it is the light that shines in the darkness, and yet only rarely is it the true light, which is life at the same time. In Christian teaching one is led into this life to begin with by means of belief: "He that believeth on the Son hath everlasting life: and he that believeth not in the Son shall not see life; but the wrath of God abideth on him" (John 3.36). This life is eternal life, free of interrupted consciousness.[36] Man experiences it, *sees* it. Its opposite is wrath, in which God's face is turned away from him. "Amen, Amen, I say unto you, He that heareth my word, and believeth on him that sent me, hath everlasting life, and shall not come into condemnation; but is passed from death unto life" (John 5.24). And likewise: "He that believeth on him — the son — is not condemned: but he that believeth not is condemned already, because he hath not believed in the name of the only begotten son of God" (John 3.18).

This life is brought about by an act of cognition: "And this is the will of him that sent me, that everyone which seeth the Son and believeth on him, may have everlasting life" (John 6.40; see also John 3.15,16; 6.47). "I am the resurrection and the life" (John 11.25); "For if ye believe not that I am, ye shall die in your sins" (John 8.24). "And this is life eternal, that they might know thee the only true God, and Jesus Christ, whom thou hast sent" (John 17.3). Light, Word, Love are the kingdom of eternal life is John's teaching in his first Epistle.

The act of cognition may take the form of the Lord's Supper. To eat the bread of life, which is the I am (John 6), or to drink from the living water (John 4.11,14), the true drink (John 6), means the same as to "hear his voice" (John 10.27) or to keep his Logos (John 8.51). Such is the Father's commandment, which means eternal life (John 12.50). The I am is the true bread of life — *alethinón* (John 6.33, 35,48). The spirit brings life. The sayings of the Logos-being are spirit and life (John 6.63,68). St. John's Gospel was written, "that ye might believe that Jesus is the Christ, the Son of God; and that believing in his name ye might have life" (John 20.31). In all the above quotations, John uses *zoé* to refer to eternal life, which is not separate from light and which is therefore a live, experienced life, an everlasting presence—*zoé*. The New Testament also uses another word for "life," *psyché*, which means soul. *Psyché* is the life that the soul depends upon and is attached to. It is the life which is normally dear to man, which he cares about. Therefore it says: "He that loveth his life—*psyché*—shall lose it; and he that hateth his life—*psyché*—in this world shall keep it unto life eternal—*eis zóen aionion*" (John 12.25 and correspondingly Matt. 16.25 and Luke 12.22). The word *psyché* is used in this sense by Matthew 6.25 and 2.20, and by Paul when he uses the word *psychikós*: "It is sown a life-body (or soul-body)"—the translation says: natural body —". . . the first man, Adam, was made a living soul—*psyché* —the last Adam an enlivening spirit" (1.Cor. 15.44-45 and similarly 1.Cor. 2.14). The distinction here is between the concept of natural life, to which the living being clings, and spiritual-eternal life, which does not belong to the being, but in which it may share.

Only in the world of life can the I am become true experience. In the world of the past, I am is the expression of the gesture of Cain, of death. This quality of death accompanies the thoughts and deeds of modern man. Through this gesture and at this price he becomes self-conscious. A hidden heroism, a hidden strength, is inherent in man in the very fact that he can live with the death within him. The devastation of nature occurs according to the same death-principle. Man and world burn in the same fire. The knowledge of the dead increases powerfully, giving rise to more and more death. A sharp, dead light lights up a more and more desolated world—a civilized, not a natural, desert.

According to the texts, everything that is essentially new

BECOMING AWARE OF THE LOGOS

in Christianity stands, in opposition to the rigid letter of the law, as life, living light, unhiddenness: the overcoming of death, of *léthe*. In the face of our contemporary consciousness we are forced to conclude that the life we know is still "without light," i.e. without conscious experience. That is, the light that we know still lacks life. The Christian impulse as regards the light of life has not yet become a reality. "I am the light of the world — I am the resurrection and the life" (John 11.25) — "I am the way, the truth and the life" (John 14.6). It is obvious how much the "I-am-here" is connected with the principle of life and light, indeed is identical with the synthesis of the two. We know this especially when the "I am the light of the world" is uttered for the first time and is followed directly by "he that followeth me shall not walk in darkness, but shall have the light of life" (John 8.12). The "light of life" is the synthesis of the two basic principles. It is not difficult to trace this theme right back to the beginning of Genesis, to the tree of life and the tree of knowledge.

This great I am saying follows the account of the adulteress who is to be stoned according to the law, and it is followed by the discussion with the Pharisees about bearing witness to oneself (John 8). The theme of "stones" appears again in the same chapter, after the saying: "Before Abraham was, I am" (John 8.58). The Jews seize stones in order to throw them at Jesus. A third time, again following an I am phrase — "I and my Father are one" — St. John says: "Then the Jews took up stones again to stone him" (John 10.31). After this, before the great deed of light and life, the raising of Lazarus, the text emphasizes: "His disciples say unto him, Master, the Jews of late sought to stone thee; and goest thou thither again?" (John 11.8). Again words about the light of the world are given in reply.

LIFE

The world of stones is certainly the extreme opposite of the world of life and of the light of life. A path of meditation leads from this theme to themes like grave, body, temple, city. We shall walk this path at a later stage. At this point, we must take another direction and move toward the origin of the division of light and life: the garden. For the stony desert of today is a result of the fact that the garden was lost and that the return to it was not accomplished. Of the forbidden tree it says in Genesis: "And out of the ground made the Lord God to grow every tree that is pleasant to the sight, and good for food; the tree of life also in the midst of the garden, and the tree of knowldege of good and evil" (Gen. 2.9); "But of the tree of the knowledge of good and evil, thou shalt not eat: for in the day that thou eatest thereof thou shalt surely die" (Gen. 2.17).

"And the woman said unto the serpent: We may eat of the fruit of the trees of the garden, but of the fruit of the tree which is in the midst of the garden, God hath said: Ye shall not eat of it, neither shall ye touch it lest ye die" (Gen. 3.2-3). These texts seem to offer something significant for an understanding of the idea of "life." Originally, man was only forbidden to eat of the "tree of knowledge of good and evil," but was not forbidden to eat "of the tree of life." *After* the creation of woman, (Gen. 2.21-23), which is preceded by the naming of the warmblooded animals (Gen. 2.19-20), the serpent approaches man. Until then, man was proof against temptation, although the prohibition had been placed upon him while he was still sexless or androgynous. The woman speaks to the serpent about *one* tree, which is "in the midst of the garden." According to the above text (Gen. 2.9), the tree of life certainly stands in the midst of the garden, but whether this is true also of the tree of knowledge remains unclear. This ambiguity is removed by what

77

emerges from a deeper contemplation of the text in question: namely, before the fall, the "two" trees were originally *one*; and that life and cognition were divided by the fall. The "and" in ". . . and the tree of knowledge . . . ," indicates unity rather than duality. One tree of life and of cognition had been created, as in Gen 1.27: "So God created man in his own image, in the image of God created he him; male and female created he them." This was before the creation of woman. Therefore the "and" here can have no divisive meaning, but must mean "at the same time." This is confirmed by the Jewish legend, according to which, when his father Adam lay dying, Seth was allowed to enter the Garden, and saw there the two trees interlaced into one.

The fall is an event of consciousness. Before the separation into the two sexes, man could not be approached by the snake, because he was one with the garden, in union with the world. This union was lost through the separation into the sexes and through the naming of the animals, which indicates that man had withdrawn from a part of the world: he was no longer "at one" with himself. The dualistic world, the seed of opposition, comes about through the fall. Because of this, the woman could *see* that it would be good to eat of the tree, that it was lovely to behold, a joyous tree, because it gave wisdom. Therefore, she could "take" the fruit, which was exactly what was forbidden. Not only eating, but touching too was forbidden (Gen. 3.3), for touching "stretching the hand out for something" (Gen 3.22), and taking it, is possible only in objectivity, in standing-over-against. Being separated from the world is the expulsion from paradise. The elaboration of this theme has a further consequence: man cannot be allowed to eternalize the state of separation and therefore has to die, in order to return, from time to time, from separated being into unity.

LIFE

The kind of knowing which does not cognize in a *living* way was internalized. Since then, man experiences himself as facing life "from the outside." He remains outside reality, outside life. With the gesture of the Ram — or the Lamb — he begins to look at what he has already thought, at the past of his own consciousness, at the "outer." This is the moment of reversal.

In the garden man was "within"; there was no outer and inner. Expulsion from it meant that he went "out" — out of life, out of reality. The path into the wilderness began. Outside the garden there is no experience of life, no presence. But in the garden man was not yet an I-being. Through the fall his attention, therefore his love, focused on himself. His mineral body moved into the center of his attention; and where his attention is, man is. What united man and being in the garden — though united is an inadequate description because, in order to be "united," one has to have been first "separated" — what made man one, was life and love. In the garden, life was still light without darkness, love was *first love*. It was not yet human love, which bridges separation, but was the love of beings higher than man; their being, their essence, weaving in living light. This light and this weaving is their being and their essence.

In a certain sense, earthly love is — in its perfection — stronger. It has to bridge what is separated, and has to arise continuously anew out of the transformation of self-love. Indeed, it only *is* in its arising. Because it is living, it can have no past. Love lives, if it is living love, always against the self-love out of which it arises.

Through love man returns again "within." Love is a fruit of living cognizing, of presence, of experienced light, the light of life. Whoever attains the light of life, establishes a unity, which was broken in primal history. Human light

—consciousness—has no life today. It rests on lightless, objectified life, the life of the body. Without the living bodily "apparatus," ordinary consciousness is impossible. Our path leads to kindling the light of consciousness into its own life. Then, in order to survive, consciousness will no longer need the corporeal instrument. It will not have to destroy the life-forces of the body in order to become conscious through what is dead.[37] Thereby the gesture of Cain will be abolished. The phrase: "He that loveth his life—*psyché*—shall lose it..." (John 12.25), must be understood in the sense that attachment to one's soul-life, the wish to feel oneself, excludes eternal life. Eternal life is living consciousness of the I-am-here, which no longer needs to support itself upon the body. It is the principle that lives behind every "I" utterance, initially making it possible and then working itself slowly up to present consciousness. Therefore one may say: the cognizer in man has eternal life. "He that hath the Son hath life" (1.John 5.12). The Son is the cognitive principle in man. The oldest way to partake of the Son is Holy Communion, the eating of bread and wine—neither of them mere products of nature but of human labor also—with the cognizing feeling that it is through the Logos that they are what they are: his body and his blood. As a purification of the eating of the forbidden fruit, "touching" eating, this cognizing eating forms the beginning of the realization: "All things were made through him, and without him was not anything made that was made." His radiance—his splendor—is the earthly world in its aliveness. Truly, he is the "Prince of life" (Acts 3.15).

SEVEN

Spirit

> Since winged delight carried you over
> many early abysses
> now build the unheard bridges'
> daring, calculable arch.
>
> The wonder is not only
> the inexplicable surviving of danger;
> wonder first becomes wonderful
> in sheer, pure, free performance.
>
> It's not presumption to cooperate
> in the undescribable relation,
> the intertwining becomes more and more
>   intimate,
> to be carried along is not enough.
>
> Your practiced forces stretch
> until they span two
> contradictions... For in man
> the God will be advised.
>
>   *Rilke*

In the beginning was the Logos. The spirit is active in anyone who can see this, who can repeat this gesture in himself.

For the old, *Vidya* consciousness,[38] the earth was still

81

light. This was a vestige of the state in which, cosmologically speaking, sun and earth were still a single heavenly body.[39] There was no outer light yet, for everything was light. Since everything was light, there was no darkness. Everything was light — from our point of view, seen with today's eyes. But the old consciousness could not experience the light — for earthly beings then there was no light. Man could not orient himself between light and darkness, earth and sun. And yet with regard to the essence of connections, the reality of relationships,[40] the old, dim, dreaming consciousness was in a certain sense much lighter and brighter than today's mirrored consciousness. But that consciousness did not experience this brightness, this light. Man did not know it as an experience, and therefore consciousness did not experience itself. For this very reason the old consciousness may be called a dreaming consciousness. Man was within the event. He was not even sufficiently outside it to experience it *as* an event.

The age which we may characterize with the words "the light in the darkness," in which it becomes possible to become aware of the light, begins only after the slow decline of this earlier epoch. With the Logos-being's appearance on the earth, the seed for the third age, the age of the spirit, is sown. Cosmologically speaking, the lightsource of consciousness begins to enter consciousness, where it will one day dwell. But up to now the source of consciousness is still outside. We do not know how and why we think the way we do; consciousness cannot account for itself.

In this second epoch, perceiving and thinking gradually separate themselves. For human beings today, thinking is undoubtedly "inside," while perceiving is "outside." This is why, on the one hand, the world of percepts has a universal character—"the sun shines for everyone"—while on the other hand it is difficult to determine that thinking is not a private business. At the very most, the production of thought is individual, but this in fact is the only individual thing about it. For contemporary man the content of perception is determined by thinking. Perception itself, however, independent of its interpretation by thinking, still flows today from pre-individual sources. Man does not feel that he produces his own perception. If man is to become a self-aware being, the shift from perceiving to thinking, from the light to the word, must occur. For man becomes free only in thinking; he awakens in the word. Then, beginning with thinking, he can extend his freedom into other fields.

Father-consciousness was an uninterrupted, dreaming light-consciousness. The Fathers—initiates who could say I—did not mean themselves by the word "I," but meant God-the-Father, the universal Godhead. For non-initiates this I word was the unspeakable name of God. Accordingly, teaching and instruction were given, not rationally by means of sentences, but through words, syllables, sounds. Just as spoken word and gesture can awaken understanding in the child, when it "learns" to speak, so words or sounds could work in earlier humanity. The "teaching" behind each word, sound, and syllable was the reality of the master who "speaks": it was his radiance, his "revelation." The syllable "AUM," for instance, was the central power in which every line of verse culminated, as in a central point, in order to submerge itself in the source of the light and to draw strength from its wholeness. In the Gospel of St. John, "Amen" is a similar all-inclusive teaching. "Amen, Amen I say unto you . . ."—*that* was the real teaching. What follows is a specification of this essential teaching, and derives its truth from it. Every

83

teaching, all art, which is to say, every picture, drama, all music is aimed at *me*. It teaches me how to achieve a free relationship to the picture, drama or teaching, even if this aim is not articulated and is known only by few. For pictures, dramas and teachings alike presuppose a receptive subject; they educate and form the subject by not compelling him, or at least not compelling him to the degree that he is "compelled" by the world of perception. To earlier humanity the world of percepts was not a "picture" world, because the power of cognition was also contained in it. Today this power lives *in us*. It was precisely through art, spiritual teaching, and culture, that man was taught to distinguish between image and reality, appearance and reality, everyday-reality and essential reality, i.e. the reality of being. A human being capable of making these distinctions has developed in order to create out of nothing a new, free relationship to the "given." The given itself also came forth out of nothing. Everything was human creation, even if given by divine inspiration and guidance. Image and drama are *only* image, *only* drama; they do not compel. They lead to the recognition that everything is image and show; that there is no compelling reality. For *me*, everything is image and show. For *me*, everything is teaching. The cognitive power, which facilitates this understanding, has been won from earlier, compelling reality and has now entered humanity.

Thus thinking consciousness is cultivated on the path of consciousness as it descends into isolation, into individuality. The ascending power now works in the world of individual parts, the world of fragmentary consciousness, twisted by the fall. It now leads downwards. The world broke open in the fall, and the force of breaking divides it into ever smaller parts. The reversal occurs at the lowest point. It is the last intervention of the Godhead, the mystery of Golgotha. The Logos-being had to show himself in the darkness, to suffer human destiny in its extremist form in order to *show* man his destiny and to bring him to the possibility of return. As every achievement must first be effected by an individual in order, later, to become a general accomplishment, so too the Logos-being was necessary for this deed of creation, in order to live out in a human form what will later be possible for all human beings.

The phrase, "the invisible God," implies a highly prepared consciousness. The history of the people of the Old Testament is partly the story of relapses into the worship of idols, symbols of the gods, particularizations of the One, that had to a great extent already lost their meaning at that time. To await the Messiah and to prepare his ways was this people's great task. At the same time, however, the understanding of the Messiah was made difficult for this people. Having finally achieved the cult of the invisible, it had to accept the appearance of the Godhead in visible, human form. After struggling against idolatry in various animal forms, the symbol for which was the golden calf, there comes the appearance of God in a human shape. The Creator of man sends his essence, his creative word, his *appearance* or *revelation*, the Man-God, in order to have the living God-Man before men (John 1.18).

This most nearly human form of the divine (the Son of *God*) draws down into the most nearly divine form of man (the Son of *Man*). Just as the snake was lifted up by Moses (Numbers 21.8), the Son of Man is lifted up (John 3.13; 8.28; 12.34). The snake, creeping on its stomach, *touching* the earth's surface with its whole body, *adhering* to the earth, became, by its being lifted from the horizontal to the vertical,

85

an image which heals man from the snakebite. The snake was lifted from the earth, out of the dust, its spinal column was raised upright like man's. Thereby what had been a curse — before its redemption the snake was the symbol of this curse — was transformed into a healing principle, which liberates from the curse. Through the exaltation of the Son of Man, man was delivered from man. It was possible for him once more to re-establish his original nature, as it had been before the fall. This was the Godhead's last act of creation. But, in the person of the Logos-bearer, man had to do his part too. The power which led man downwards — through every teaching, independent of its content — was reversed by this exaltation, creating the possibility of striving upwards.

Every temple, every sanctuary, every idol, every offering is a token of man's struggle to bring his divinity closer to the earth, that it may live "amongst us" and appear in human form. Every myth, every teaching, every story of the gods, of Brahman and Atman, is an attempt to bring man to self-consciousness, to the experience of his I, so that he may achieve divine consciousness.

The earth, "this world" is a human reality, a reality of human consciousness. The world is as man *sees* it; it is *how* he sees. It is not caused by the arbitrariness of mirrored consciousness, for *how* man sees it is determined primarily by cosmic and divine activity, and — since the last deed of creation — also by human and cosmic activities. The history of human cognitive consciousness and the history of the earth — including its physical-cosmic environment — are *one* history.

Through the separation of the sun from the earth,[41] the source of light withdrew, and departed from human con-

SPIRIT

sciousness. For human consciousness to have the source of its light in itself means, in a cosmic sense, that the sun must re-unite with the earth. Now we see the light in darkness, mirrored by darkness, "... for now we see through a glass..." (1.Cor. 13.12). Cosmologically speaking, we see the light mirrored by the moon, the exhausted, dead part of consciousness. The beginning of the Sun's return is the dwelling of the Logos in man.

The appearance of the Logos was still a divine act, and inasmuch as it was, it could easily have disturbed man in his development towards freedom, so providing the sequence: first, the invisible, then, transitorily the visible Son, and now, finally, a humanity abandoned by God. True, no God appears visibly any longer. Instead, the Son sends the "Comforter-Spirit," the third Divine Person, the invisible Divinity who can act in man.

The Son therefore must leave the world of visibility: "Nevertheless I tell you the truth; It is expedient for you that I go away: for if I go not away, the Comforter will not come unto you; but if I depart, I will send him unto you" (John 16.7; also compare John 7.39).

To experience the Logos as perception is the Son. To experience the Logos as inner power is the Spirit.

If the attention turns to the Logos, to cognition, then the Spirit is the power of seeing it. To see the Logos is the first real activity of the Spirit. "In the beginning was the Logos." It is the spirit, the power of knowing the Logos that realizes this experience in man.

The Son is the Father's countenance or word, but the ability to see him is the Spirit: the Logos in me. As a visible experience the Son would simply extinguish human I-consciousness. This is what happened to the man, Jesus, who sacrificed his I-consciousness for the Logos. This is what also happened to the disciples. Up to the arrest of Jesus, the Logos penetrated them like a luminous enchantment. His essence spread amongst them and spoke through them. At the moment of the arrest this enchantment ended: the disciples fled. Otherwise it would be imcomprehensible why Judas had to "betray" him, point him out to the officers — after all, he had openly taught daily in the temple. But, because the Logos-being spoke now through one disciple, now through another, outsiders could not know, which one of them he was. Thus he says, at the hour of leave-taking, "Behold, the hour cometh, yea is now come, that ye shall be scattered, every man into his own and shall leave me alone" (John 16.32). Into their own: the disciples return from being permeated by the Logos into their own being — *eis tá ídia* — into their own consciousness.

In the plant, minerality or the mineral form of existence is overcome. In the animal, both the mineral and plant forms of existence are overcome. In each case the highest principle determines the outer appearance: in the animal, it is the "form of sensitivity" according to its species; in the plant it is the living form. In man, everyday I consciousness — mirrored I-consciousness — is generally determinative. The entrance of the higher I extinguishes this consciousness and determines its own form of existence. In the drama played out between the Godhead and man, human consciousness was partly lost, even among those around the Logos-bearer. Thereafter only the spirit in its invisible form can lead one into freedom: "Ye shall know the truth, and the truth shall make you free" (John 8.32). "The Spirit of truth," however, is the Comforter: "Howbeit when he, the Spirit of truth, is come, . . ." (John 16.13); "But when the Com-

SPIRIT

forter is come, whom I will send unto you from the Father, the Spirit of truth, . . ." (John 15.26); "And I will pray the Father, and he shall give you another Comforter, that he may abide with you forever, the Spirit of truth . . ." (John 14.16). Paul says likewise: "Now the Lord is that Spirit: and where the Spirit of the Lord is, there is liberty" (2.Cor 3.17).

"Spirit of truth" means the new human ability to find the truth, that which is otherwise hidden, out of oneself and independently of all perception. The Logos, through whom all things became, is in this spirit: he knows all things. Thus St. John writes: "But ye have an unction from the Holy One, and ye know all things" (1.John 2.10). "But the anointing which ye have received of him abideth in you, and ye need not that any man teach you: but as the same anointing teacheth you of all things, and is truth, and is no lie, and even as it hath taught you, ye shall abide in him" (1.John 2.27).

This ability appears in man like a primal power of knowing everything. Accordingly the Gospel says: "Howbeit when he, the Spirit of truth, is come, he will guide you into all truth: for he shall not speak of himself; but whatsoever he shall hear, that shall he speak: and he will show you things to come" (John 16.13). Paul writes even more clearly: "But God hath revealed them unto us by his Spirit: for the Spirit searcheth all things, yea, the deep things of God" (1.Cor. 2.10). It almost sounds like *Anámnesis*, Plato's theory of universal memory, when we read in St. John: "But the Comforter, which is the Holy Ghost, whom the Father will send in my name, he shall teach you all things, and bring all things to your remembrance, whatsoever I have said unto you" (John 14.26).

It is difficult to understand how religious agnosticism,

89

the teaching that religious truths were closed forever to human knowledge, could arise in the Middle Ages, since the quoted passages stand in open contradiction to the assumption of any limits to cognition — quite apart from the fact that the revelation, to which we owe otherwise unapproachable truths, had to be received by men, and therefore had to be cognized in order to exist at all as a revelation for mankind. The assumption of a revelation occurring independently of cognition corresponds unmistakably to the idea then being developed of a material reality, existing independently of cognition, which is today man's underlying conception and feeling, and determines everything else.

In modern times, the ability to produce the truth out of oneself is revealed in the abstract capacity to work out the truths of mathematics and pure physics quite independently of sense-perception and experiment. This procedure — which may be traced back to Newton originally — produced the conceptual scaffolding and outlook fundamental to all the natural sciences. Such pure thinking, if applied to other fields, could create the possiblitiy of thinking with mathematical precision about spiritual realities. Thereby the activity of the Spirit in man would truly begin. Awareness of the Logos could be kindled by pure thinking about the light of consciousness. Perceiving the Logos, the spirit could assume its true function: to investigate the obstacles which stand in the way of realizing consciousness-in-the-present, and to develop methods for removing these. For the spirit of the Comforter does not yet *dwell* in man. To dwell and to remain are *one* word in Greek: *ménein*. To remain, in the Greek sense, meant: *enduring presence*, real living, not just "visiting." In modern man, the spirit acts, so to speak, like a "visitor." Through intellectual intuition man can grasp the concepts of the Ram, such as idea, thinking, living thinking, conceiving. But, since the intuition does not remain, but blazes up and goes out, man does not *live*, i.e. experience, the spirit which is active in the intellectual intuition. The spirit's remaining or dwelling would be an experience which continues in time. It would mean that one *remains* in the spirit, that one *lives* in the "super-wordly" realm, in living thinking, i.e. in *life*. Therefore the Gospel says: "And I will pray the Father, and he shall give you another Comforter, that he may abide with you forever: the spirit of truth; whom the world cannot receive, because it seeth him not, neither knoweth him: but ye know him; for he dwelleth — *ménei* — with you, and shall be in you" (John 14.16-17). The spirit lives with the disciples who have cognized the Son: they see the spirit. This makes more comprehensible the sayings in the Epistle: "... but as the same anointing teacheth you of all things, ... ye shall abide in it" (1.John 2.27). "And he that keepeth his commandments dwelleth in him, and he in him. And thereby know we that we dwell in him, and he in us, because he hath given us of his spirit" (1.John 4.13).

The Trinity is the threefold revelation of the One, of God. Jehovah represents simultaneously the Father, the Son and the Spirit. Humanly speaking, there are three aspects. The divine power which works independently of human cognition, and also within cognition, is the Father. The divine power which reveals the Father, and receives this revelation in man, is the Son. And the Comforter, the God who can awaken in human consciousness insofar as it becomes aware of the Logos, is the Spirit. Thus the Gospel states with regard to the Spirit: "He shall glorify — transfigure — me: for he shall receive of mine, and shall shew it unto you.

BECOMING AWARE OF THE LOGOS

All things that the Father hath are mine: therefore said I, that he shall take of mine, and shall shew it unto you" (John 16.14-15). The direct consequence of this is: "I will not leave you comfortless: I will come to you. Yet a little while, and the world seeth me no more; but ye see me: because I live ye shall live also. At that day ye shall know that I am in my Father, and ye in me, and I in you" (John 14.18-20).

The Spirit is *Comforter* insofar as he comes to the disciples who have been left as "orphans." After the ascension of the Logos-being the disciples lose their Comforter forever from the perceptual sphere, now become the desert of "this world" (John 16.10). The disciples' sadness before Pentecost is part of the pentecostal miracle, the most significant aspect of which is that, right away, the apostles understood the event in full consciousness. Peter's words make this quite clear (Acts 2.14-15).

The spirit is breathed on those who cognize the Logos (John 20.22). This is the second creation of man, following the first creation and "breathing" (Gen. 2.7). Paul refers to this second "breathing": ". . . The first man Adam was made a living soul; the last Adam was made a quickening spirit" (1.Cor. 15.45); "But ye are not in the flesh, but in the Spirit, if so be that the Spirit of God dwell in you. Now if any man have not the Spirit of Christ, he is none of his" (Romans 8.9; compare also Acts 5.32). The idea of the spirit undergoes a further development in Paul, connected with a metamorphosis of the idea of the children of God (Romans 8). The spirit is concealed in every man. However, in concealment, it does not become the spirit of truth, of un-concealment — *alétheia* — but turns against itself, becoming the power by which *denial* becomes possible — denial of the Word, of the Spirit, of the Father. All depends on man. The power is

92

SPIRIT

there. "Now he which establisheth us with you in Christ, and hath anointed us, is God; who hath also sealed us, and given the earnest of the Spirit in our hearts" (2.Cor. 1.21-22). This power works itself up in order to become active in us and in the world. If we do not help it reach this aim, it will work in us through destiny and difficulties, suffering and illness. If we strive in the sense of the Spirit, it will help us by means of intuitions: "Likewise the Spirit also helpeth our infirmities: for we know not what we should pray for as we ought: but the Spirit itself maketh intercession for us with groanings which cannot be uttered" (Romans 8.26). The apocalyptic beast is the reverse of this impulse of the Spirit (Rev. 13).

Through the indwelling of the Logos the capacity of cognition has been given to us. The possibility of cognizing God means the beginning of the third age, the Age of the Spirit. Cognition of God is cognition of the light within the light: a speaking world. John condenses this in the words: "And we know that the Son of God is come, and hath given us an understanding, that we may know him that he is true, and we are in him that is true, even in his Son Jesus Christ. This is the true God, and eternal life. Little Children, keep yourselves from idols. Amen" (1.John 5.20-21).

We could continue with the words of Paul: Keep yourselves from "... dumb idols" (1.Cor. 12.2), from an idol-like, mute, wordless world — a world pictured without the Logos.

EIGHT

God's Dwelling: The Temple-City

> As the watchman in the vineyards
> has his hut and watches,
> I am a hut in your hands, O Lord,
> I am night, O Lord, of your night.
>
> Vineyard, pasture, ancient apple-orchard,
> field that never misses a spring,
> fig tree, in marble soil,
> bearing fruit in hundreds:
>
> Scent rises from your round branches.
> You do not ask whether I awake;
> fearless, released in saps,
> your depths rise silently past me.
> *Rilke*

The Spirit in man which sees the Logos is the most individualized form of the Godhead. It is what human beings have most in common with each other and is thus what can unite them, now that, after thousands of years of isolation, they are free. The waves of the creative Word must ebb in "this" world, and the Logos itself must die in this world and die for it. For the Godhead no longer creates in this world, which is precisely why it *is* this world. The fate of the Logos-being in man is the same: the history of the world and the history of consciousness are one and the same. Insofar as the cognizer in man, the one who comes from above, acts in the body, the living thought must die at the end of the process of consciousness. But the kernel of human consciousness, coming from above, still lives in darkness, as if asleep. And this one who lives looks on the death of the Logos in consciousness as on his own past: he perceives he is alive. As far as he becomes conscious of this perception, realizing in a true and conscious manner the gesture of the Ram, he himself begins to guide the process. Awakening the spirit awakens both itself and the resurrection of dead thinking, of the Word, of the Son, of the world.[42]

To become aware of the Godhead in a human body presented the greatest difficulty for the members of the Chosen People. As a people, they did not understand what played out before their eyes, although their entire history was a preparation for it. No *people* could have understood it; only individuals could more or less have grasped it. To understand it is a completely individual act, for which membership in a people or community is no help. One may even suspect that the Chosen People as a whole *had* to fail, since had they understood, the death of the Logos-bearer would not have occurred and all the possibilities for human development brought about by this death would be lacking. For this death to occur, an individual as well as a community had to cooperate.

This people had earned the One, the Invisible. He is a special God, the one who addresses the man, Moses, at whose request he speaks his name. He chooses his people and desires to dwell with them: "And let them make me a sanctuary; that I may dwell among them" (Exodus 25.8). More precisely, it is written of Solomon's Temple: "Then there shall

BECOMING AWARE OF THE LOGOS

be a place which the Lord your God shall choose to cause his name to dwell there, ..." (Deut. 12.11; compare Deut. 14.23 and 1.Kings 8.48). This is the descent of the Godhead among men: first, the moveable tabernacle of God; then the sanctuary in Jerusalem, wherein dwells the Invisible One, his Name. Therefore it is all too easy to understand that it is experienced as blasphemy when the Godhead now appears in a visible form, in a human body. But the Chosen People do not recognize the *name* in this form. After the saying, "I and the Father are one," there follows the "explanation": "For a good work we stone thee not; but for blasphemy; and because that thou, being a man, makest thyself God. Jesus answered them, Is it not written in your law, I said, Ye are gods? If he called them gods, unto whom *the word of God* came, and the scripture cannot be broken; Say ye of him, whom the Father hath sanctified, and sent into the world, Thou blasphemest; because I said: I am the Son of God?" (John 10. 33-36). Man is already God in that God's Word speaks to him. But, for the Jews, God lives in Solomon's Temple. With regard to this, the Logos-bearer announces a change: "... the hour cometh, when ye shall neither in this mountain, nor yet at Jerusalem, worship the Father ... But the hour cometh, and now is, when the true worshippers shall worship the Father in spirit and in truth: for the Father seeketh such to worship him. God is a spirit: and they that worship him must worship him in spirit and in truth" (John 4.21-24). The breath of the spirit is palpable. Something similar, but on a more human plane, may be found in St. Matthew's Gospel: "But thou, when thou prayest, enter into thy closet, and when thou hast shut thy door, pray to thy Father which is in secret; and thy Father which seeth in secret shall reward thee openly" (Matt. 6.6).

Clearly, a new form of worship is being prepared. The

GOD'S DWELLING: THE TEMPLE-CITY

destruction of the sanctuary in Jerusalem — predicted by the Logos-bearer (Luke 21.6; Mark 13.2; Matt. 24.2) — occurs in accordance with this. At the same time the theme of the destruction of the temple is connected with the destruction of the human body, which — according to the words of the Logos-bearer — can be raised up again in three days (John 2.19-21; Matt. 26.61; Mark 14.58; 15.29). Spoken thus by the Logos-bearer himself, the statement occurs only in St. John's Gospel. St. Matthew and St. Mark do not quote it directly, but only report persons who refer to it — false witnesses and those who mock the crucified one. This indicates the unity of the Gospels.

That body and sanctuary, as also body and city, can represent each other, stems from ancient traditions. Already in the Upanishads the body is called the city of *Atman*, of *Brahman*. It has 11 (or 9) gates — openings of the body — while Ezekiel (Ez. 48.31-34) and the Apocalypse (Rev. 21.12-13) describe the city with 12 gates. Moreover in Hebrew tradition the second letter *beth* or *bes* signifies man's sheath, whether it be his bodily sheath, his house, tent, or sanctuary. It is man's sheath that separates him from his various surroundings, thereby making cognition possible on every level. "In this world" the physical body is the sheath; however, on higher planes of cognition, still finer sheaths or "huts" must be built by man himself. This is how we must understand the words of Peter in the transfiguration scene (Matt. 17.4; Mark 9.5; Luke 9.33). His sheaths allow man to become independent.

In the temptation scene, the image of the city is used to refer to the bodily sheath (Matt. 4.5; Luke 4.9).

The one who is to come (John 1.15,27,30; 3.31; 6.14; 11.27; Matt. 26.64), the *Erchoménos*, the God who comes from on high, the awaited Messiah, is to be found on his way to mankind in Solomon's sanctuary. Then he draws even closer. The theme of "from above" is often touched on in the Fourth Gospel. In chapter 3 it is written, "Amen, Amen I say unto you, unless one is born from above, one cannot see the kingdom of heaven..." (John 3.3), and "Do not be astonished that I told you: It is necessary that you are born from above" (John 3.7). And, in the same chapter, the Baptist says: "He that cometh from above is above all: he that is of the earth is earthly, and speaketh of the earth: he that cometh from heaven is above all" (John 3.31). The Logos-being himself testifies that he comes from heaven (John 6.38). He is the bread that has come down from heaven (John 6.50). In the crucial discourse in Chapter 8 he says: "Ye are from beneath, I am from above..." (John 8.23). The Prologue also, of course, describes the descent of the Logos to his new place: "And he came and dwelt among us" — (literally, "and he placed his tent within us" — (John 1.14). For John the dwelling of the Logos in a human body is of central importance: "That which was from the beginning, which we have heard, which we have seen with our eyes, which we have looked upon, and our hands have touched, of the Word of life..." (1.John 1.1).

The new sanctuary is man himself — initially, the body of the Logos-bearer. But, as the Gospel continues there are more and more references to dwelling — remaining — and to the mansions of the Father. The promises in John 14.3,12,14 among others, especially the greatest promise, the promise of the spirit, point to the event of Pentecost, to the appearance of the Logos and his indwelling in several men as personal and super-personal spirit (John 14.16-25).

For this reason the Logos himself and his sayings are to "remain," to be preserved. The word "remaining" or "dwelling" appears in the first chapter of St. John's Gospel in words whose meaning can only be guessed at. Luther, and the King James version to a lesser degree, express this in the language and images of everyday life: "Then Jesus turned and saw them — the two disciples of the Baptist — following and saith unto them, What seek ye? They said unto him, Rabbi, (which is to say, being interpreted, Master,) where dwellest — livest — thou?" Luther translates this: "Where are you staying" — "He saith unto them, Come and see. They came and saw where he dwelt — was staying — and abode with him that day: for it was about the tenth hour" (John 1.38-39). The last sentence shows that it was not a visit in the ordinary sense. When he addresses the Jews, the Logos-being says: "... And ye have not his (the Father's) word abiding in you ..." (John 5.38), which also describes the state of contemporary human consciousness: We can think, thanks to the power of the Logos, but we can only "dwell" in the already-thought, not in the process of thinking itself. This, however, is precisely the quality and condition characteristic of the true disciple: "If you remain in my word, then you are truly my disciples" (John 8.31). "Remaining" means maintaining the connection with the spiritual source: "I am the vine, ye are the branches: He that abideth in me, and I in him, the same bringeth forth much fruit: for without me ye can do nothing" (John 15.5). When the new commandment is repeated, first the theme of "remaining" is elaborated: "As the Father hath loved me, so have I loved you: continue ye in my love. If ye keep my commandments, ye shall abide in my love; even as I kept my Father's commandments, and abide in his love" (John 15.9-10). This is condensed in John's first Epistle: "Let that therefore abide in you, which ye have heard from the beginning. If that which ye have heard from the beginning shall remain in you, ye also shall continue in the Son and in the Father" (1.John 2.24). To see the Son is the first step; next comes remaining in Him: "Whosoever abideth in him sinneth not: whosoever sinneth has not seen him, neither known him" (1.John 3.6).

"Remaining" means continuity in higher consciousness; it is life in this higher sphere, in contrast to returning into one's individual existence, *eis tá ídia* or "into one's house" (e.g. John 7.53). This is most clearly shown in St. Peter's conversation with the risen one: "Peter seeing him (the beloved disciple) saith to Jesus, Lord, and what shall this man do? Jesus saith unto him, If I will that he tarry till (while) I come, what is that to thee? follow thou me. Then went this saying abroad among the brethren, that that disciple should not die: yet Jesus said not unto him, 'he shall not die'; but, If I will that he tarry till I come, what is that to thee?" (John 21.21-23).

Remaining (tarrying) in the Logos or holding the Logos (John 8.31 and 51) means that the inner light does not fade, that *alétheia* is not "forgotten," and that the "life" does not die. Moreover, through the maintaining of the Logos, love also becomes perfect: "But whoso keepeth his (the Lord's) word, in him verily (*alethós*: without interruption) is the love of God perfected" (1.John 2.5). Similarly, the Logos-bearer himself says: "If a man love me, he will keep my word—*logos*—and my Father will love him, and we will come unto him, and make our abode with him" (John 14.23). The disciples are promised that they will dwell with the Father: "In my Father's house are many mansions (dwellings)" (John 14.2). Individuality is preserved within this spiritual sphere. As was said earlier, each person requires a "mansion" for his cognitive existence.

GOD'S DWELLING: THE TEMPLE-CITY

The Gospels, particularly the Fourth Gospel, lead us to the entry of the Logos-God into a human body and promise the coming of the Spirit, which is to teach all things and to lead to every truth. The outer sanctuary is destroyed. The Godhead now "dwells" in men in its third form. Dwelling means that a person affirms the fact that he is chosen; for in the Age of the Spirit all men are chosen, otherwise the spirit would merely flare up within and turn against itself and against man, driving him unwittingly into a suicidal stance in which he would deny his humanity, his spiritual being, with the help of the spirit. The later texts of the New Testament describe the Spirits' dwelling in its new sanctuary more thoroughly. The Acts of the Apostles tells of the "miraculous" event of Pentecost, but does so in the full light of consciousness; the Epistles and the Apocalypse tell of the new temple. "Ye are God's husbandry, ye are God's building," writes St. Paul (1.Cor. 3.9). "Know ye not that ye are the temple of God, and that the Spirit of God dwelleth in you?" (1.Cor. 3.16), and more precisely: "What? know ye not that your body is the temple of the Holy Ghost which is in you, which ye have of God, and ye are not your own?" (1.Cor. 6.19).

The following passages are the foundation-stones of Christian Freemasonry: "And ye are built upon the foundation of the apostles and prophets, Jesus Christ himself being the chief cornerstone; In whom all the building fitly framed together groweth unto an holy temple in the Lord: In whom ye are also builded together for an habitation of God through the Spirit" (Eph. 2.20-22). — "To whom coming, as unto a living stone, disallowed indeed of men, but chosen of God, and precious; Ye also, as lively stones, are built up a spiritual house, an holy priesthood . . ." (1.Peter 2.4-8).

Clearly, the idea of the temple not built by human hands

was alive in early Christianity. It may be traced back to St. Mark's Gospel where the false witnesses say: "We heard him say, I will destroy this temple that is made with hands, and within three days I will build another made without hands" (Mark 14.58). St. Paul points to this temple: "For we know that if our earthly house of this tabernacle were dissolved, we have a building of God, an house not made with hands, eternal in the heavens" (2.Cor. 5.1; Hebr. 9,11,24). Equally alive was the idea that the *city* meant not only the human body, but also the habitations of men or, more exactly, the final goal of human beings, whose path leads from the garden through the desert into the city. All that man has added to nature—all culture, civilization, technology—is designated by the term *city*. For the Jews and for the inhabitants of Palestine *the city* was Jerusalem, whose heart was *the temple*. The idea of the city also meant human community, humans living together, and the human ability to do so. If one understands the human being as a Logos-being, then one may say: there is no such thing as one man, a *single* man has no reality, for his humanity is realized only through *the word*, and this requires all of humanity, which shares the word communally. This is what is meant by the term *city*.

The city, Jerusalem, was built of stones. Just after the stones have been praised, the text says, "There shall not be left here one stone upon another" (Matt. 24.2; Mark 13.2; Luke 21.5-6). The city of the human body is likewise built of what belongs to the kingdom of the prince of this world, and its building is done from the bottom up. In earlier times a city only appeared to be built from the bottom up. Building, and even the plan of a city, were sacred acts, as we are told of the founding of Rome, not to mention the description of the temple, precise in its minutest details and directions (Ex. 25-27; 1.Kings 6-7; 2.Chron. 3-4). It can be said, with reference to the holy instructions, that these cities, this sanctuary, were built from above. Nor did the human body come about by accident; strict lawfulness was at work in the pairing of the ancestors. This can be seen paradigmatically in the family tree of Jesus. Prophecies about the Messiah always relate to the tribe of Jesse, and this is confirmed by the genealogies in St. Matthew and St. Luke. But even foreign, non-Jewish blood may be included in the preparation for a particular body, contrary to custom and law — See the Book of Ruth.

But at the time of the events in Palestine all direction "from above" was withdrawn, both as to the building and to the bringing forth of the human body. Building began to be "from below," that is, according to everyday conceptions. In the case of marriages no thought was given to descendants, because the insight for this as well as inspiration from destiny were mostly lacking. In this way, the meaning of existence and of human life, previously given from above, was lost; and in its place another "meaning" was found, appropriate to the psychological and physical man: a meaning determined from below, the striving for what is "good-for-me," good for the soul bound to the body. Our whole civilization has grown up on the principle of satisfying natural and artificial bodily, and the correspondingly psychological, needs.

This evolution reaches its culmination in theories according to which everything higher has evolved from what is lower. According to these, what is lower is the true origin. Man is assumed to have evolved from the animal, the animal from the lower species, and the living from the life-less.

Thinking is thought to be a "product" of the brain, what is spiritual a result of the soul, what is psychological a result of the biological. According to this view, evolution occurs without a plan. It is determined, on the one hand, by chance, on the other hand, by certain principles like the struggle for existence in which the most adapted survives to transmit its better qualities to his offspring. Thus the body grows "from the bottom up." It seems to escape the attention of thinkers that these principles, e.g. "the will to live," which supposedly bring about evolution, already contain anthropomorphic elements. It is not clear, given the law of inertia, which is considered to be valid, or the principle of statistical disorder, why a living being "wills" to live. From principles such as these one cannot establish the source of the principle of the "will for life." The theory of evolution from below, the development of the higher from the lower, is, nevertheless, verified by its effects: man behaves accordingly. The consequences of this include: Marxist views on the fundamental reality of economic life; Freudian views on the fundamental reality of instinctual life; Jungian views on the fundamental reality of the collective unconscious; and materialism in general with its dependence on the fundamental reality of lifeless "matter." The subject, who cognizes everything, is "forgotten." These theories can give no information regarding the origin of the relative "order" of the world—an order now supposedly tending to ever greater disorder, dying away from the primal "big bang."

At first, it may sound surprising that all these scientific viewpoints are related to those "spiritual" or religious worldviews which know neither the idea of the Son or the Logos, nor the idea of the Holy Spirit. According to these, man and the world are created by God, have emerged out of

GOD'S DWELLING: THE TEMPLE-CITY

God; but man himself is empty of the divine, or the divine is seen as mere reflection in him: he himself is not—even potentially—divine. If a divine spirit does not dwell in man, man is not a Logos-being in the active sense; he is a part of nature. In which case, he has no responsibility, everything "happens" to him, and he has no share in the divine capacity for primal beginning, for creation out of nothing. The individual man is not immortal but gives back his "rational soul" to the Godhead. The prototype of such "spiritual" teaching is orthodox Islam. But basically Christianity, too, has already, even to some extent prior to Mohammed, long been "Islamicized." It has no clear idea of the Son, and does not know the cosmic, creative and cognitive significance of the Logos. As soon as the idea of the Son and the Spirit are lost, or if they do not appear at all, as in Islam, the idea of freedom is inconceivable.

The writer of the Apocalypse calls such building of the universe "from below" the *beast*, the principle which makes an animal out of man; not a natural animal, but a human beast striving to satisfy its corrupted, unnatural instincts with the aid of its intelligence. In contrast to building the universe and the corporeal being "from below," the Apocalypse gives us the image of the city, which descends from God, out of heaven (Rev. 21.2). Paul too knows this city: "But Jerusalem, which is above, is free, which is the mother of us all" (Gal. 4.26). This city is mentioned in the Epistle to the Hebrews as an ancient tradition: "For he—Abraham —looked for a city which hath foundations, whose builder and maker is God" (Hebr. 11.10); "But now they desire a better country, that is, an heavenly: wherefore God is not ashamed to be called their God: for he hath prepared for them a city" (Hebr. 11.1; compare Hebr. 12.22). The phrase

105

"in my father's house are many mansions" (John 14.2) refers to the heavenly Jerusalem.

In a Christian sense, building from above implies developing in oneself the ability to understand what "from above" really means. This begins with the contemplation of the Logos: In the beginning was the Logos. He descends. He becomes flesh and "dwells"—pitches his tent—among us. We behold his revelation. He dwells in us with his gifts: *cháris* and *alétheia*. Now we can act as temples of the Spirit, as sons of the *living* God in the sense of "from above," because we are given the potential to cognize this meaning —*alétheia*—and the ability of moral intuition—*cháris*.

In contrast to a theory of evolution which indicates development from below upwards, St. John teaches that he who was the First, the Logos, is the Last, and appears in a human form. He passes through death as the first of those who maintain a spiritual, uninterrupted consciousness, i.e. of those whose existence is not tied to their earthly house (2.Peter 1.13), whose life is not lacking light. He is the first to be born of the dead (Col. 1.18; Rev. 1.5; Acts 26.23; 1.Cor. 15.20). His true disciples follow his example, especially John, who "tarries" (John 21.22).

The God who is to come, the *Erchoménos*, has not only come to this earth, into this world, into visibility. His path goes further: into the human tent or house. In the Old Testament he was still described as an exterior God, and in the New Testament he is also portrayed in an external appearance. In the New Testament the entry of the Logos-spirit into one who offers it a dwelling, is still described from without. The entry of the Holy Spirit is only prophesied and represented. Educated and well versed in knowledge of the outer God, the Jewish people could neither understand

GOD'S DWELLING: THE TEMPLE-CITY

nor inwardly reproduce this step at that time. Only the uneducated and ignorant were able to get an inkling of it.

Christian mystics, especially Tauler and Eckhart, *experienced* the inner God. In today's Christianity there are few who know and strive for this central point of the transformation of consciousness.

The city which is "built from above" designates the human body, which is now formed through the baptism with the spirit and the fire. At the same time the "city" stands for the living together of a new humanity on earth, as awaited by the prophets (Isaiah 60-61; Ezekiel 48). For man is real only in a "city." In that city, however, no outer light will shine any more (Rev. 22.5; 21.31; Isaiah 60.20); the inner sun in man, the Lord, God, will illuminate it. This is the final aim of life on earth: new heaven, new earth, a transparent "spiritual earth," the *Terra Lucida* of the Manicheans. The Logos has gone through visibility and entered the invisibility of the human heart; from this place he enlightens the world. The true light has entered its true temple.

NINE

The Church

> When slowly out of the already forgotten
> something once experienced rises up within us,
> clearly mastered, mild, unmeasured,
> living in the unfathomable:
>
> There the word begins as we conceive it;
> its value quietly reaches far beyond us.
> For the spirit, who makes us solitary,
> must be fully certain in order to unite us.
>
> *Rilke*

With the event in Palestine the true light entered its true temple. The expression, city "built from above," refers not only to a human society on earth that consists of individuals but also to the human individual who bears within his earthly body the spiritual seed. It follows from the view of man as a Logos-being, a thinking-speaking being, that the individual alone can never be fully human: only in community can he realize his Logos-existence. Thus—and only thus—can anthropology become a truly human science, and guidelines for the integration of the individual become a concern for the fulfillment of the age, a universal-human concern. Here lies the great difference between the aims of pre-Christian "paths" and those of thinkers since the time of Christ: the

THE CHURCH

former seek the individual salvation of the chosen, while the latter think in terms of humanity as a whole — for example, the greatest possible good for the greatest number. In practice, however, the reverse seems to be the case: in earlier cultures man lived in community, while in the epoch of Christianity he becomes more and more isolated, living almost exclusively for his own interests.

As Christianity has progressed, the question of man's and the earth's true goal has been less and less frequently raised. At the beginning stood the tradition of the New Testament, which was followed by St. Augustine's *Civitas Dei* or City of God. This widely influenced both the earthly and spiritual views of the church. But even this term — *Civitas Dei* — became profane as the knowledge of the essence of Christianity as a Logos-teaching faded. It reappeared with revolutionary emphasis in Joachim di Fiore, and was declared heretical by the church. When the spirit in man is denied, as it was by the Council of Constantinople in 869, the basis for the formation of a community — *civitas* — is lacking. Religious communities endured, however, because their cultural center was initially little affected by such doctrines and aberrations from the truth. As long as man in his inner being experiences his dependence and the pressing-in-of the "upper darkness" (it is dark to him), he seeks the place and time where communion with the source of his being, his consciousness, is nurtured. This monastic experience of community distanced itself more and more from "this world," i.e. the earthly sphere of experience. Only utopians and those who could only think in economic, material terms about the earth, because they had lost their image of man, gave any thought to an earthly future and destination.[43] These considered and still consider man only as an economic entity. Even today the best of those who care about the future of the earth and humanity think the same. In practice, however, it becomes all the time more obvious that such proposals can only be realized if human beings change their "mentality." This basically means that humanity must give up the principle of "egoism" as the foundation of all intentionality and begin not only to think but also to act on a truly human basis. The inspiration of the Old Testament prophets already shows that one's disposition of soul and one's spiritual attitude are essential aspects in the representation of the "fulfillment of the age." What strikes us immediately from their activity is that no outer compulsion or force, no external teaching, can be effective during the phase of world evolution in which the perfection of man in relation to community is supposed to take place. In the words of Isaiah: "And all thy children shall be taught of the Lord" (Isaiah 54.13); Jeremiah is even clearer: "And they shall teach no more every man his neighbor, and every man his brother, saying, Know the Lord: for they shall all know me, from the least of them unto the greatest of them" (Jer. 31.34). In the Book of Enoch we read: "On that day my chosen one will sit on the throne of glory . . . and the dwellings of those who are chosen will be countless . . ." (En. 54.34.). In the Fourth Gospel the text states with reference to the prophets: "It is written in the prophets, And they shall be all taught of God" (John 6.45). In the future, however, it is the Spirit, who will teach "all things." "But the Comforter, which is the Holy Ghost, whom the Father will send in my name, he shall teach you all things, and bring all things to your remembrance, whatsoever I have said unto you" (John 14.26). "But the anointing which ye have received of him abideth in you, and ye need not that any man teach you . . ." (1.John 2.27).

THE CHURCH

The transformation whereby man becomes a "son" or *the* man occurs through the indwelling of the Spirit, as was described in Chapter 7. The corresponding passages of the New Testament show that this indwelling is reciprocal. It is alluded to by the phrase "you in me and I in you": "At that day ye shall know that I am in my Father, and ye in me, and I in you" (John 14.20). (See also John 17.21, and the passages quoted in Chapter 7, 1.John 3.24 and 4.13). St. Paul expresses this reciprocity as knowledge: "Now I know in part; but then shall I know even as also I am known" (1.Cor. 13.12). In the same Epistle he says: "But if any man love God, the same is known of him" (1.Cor. 8.3), while in the Epistle to the Galatians he says: "But now, after that ye have known God, or rather are known of God . . ." (Gal. 4.9). A medieval mystic, Meister Eckhart, said: "The eye whereby I see God, is the eye whereby God sees me." I will know as I am known. Images and sounds of higher cognition are not moved and called into appearance by me, I only free the stage and purify it through my preparedness. Living thinking, cognizing feeling, is quickened and stirred by higher beings, "not I. . . ." It is these beings who teach the child to speak and think, who "instruct" it. Such beings "think" whole languages — like French, for example. Behind them stands the Word, the Logos-being, the inspirer of humanity's wordless speech. In cognition the human I identifies itself with pictures, tones and "words," or, more precisely, it experiences its everlasting identity with these. In this way man is "thought" or "known" by the beings who stand behind the pictures and tones. Here duality ends. The essence of the hierarchies is pure light, the light of consciousness, within which they mutually interpenetrate each other. As a Logos- or light-being, man's higher consciousness is also permeated by their light. In order to be able to bear this permeation and yet be free, man's consciousness is separated from this higher light by means of the reflection — or mirroring — of the physical body which serves as his instrument.

In this context, the word *ménein* (to remain, to dwell), receives another significance; it means "to remain consciously" "to dwell consciously." Man does not dwell consciously in his bodily tent. He is neither conscious of his true I-Being, nor does he know how he lives in his body; he does not permeate it consciously. However, as his consciousness increases, he can penetrate in an ever more deeply conscious manner down into his organism. At the turning-point of time, the path of the evolution of consciousness is characterized by terms which are difficult to understand today, and are therefore controversial. The people of the Old Testament call themselves after their worthiest representative, the "Children of Abraham" (Matt. 3.9; Luke 3.8; John 8.33 and 39). The life-creating knowledge given to Abraham, the chosen one, as a result of his striving for inspiration, remained for generations the chief concern of his family and tribe. After their liberation from Egypt by Moses the Hebrews became the chosen *people*. Until then, their human existence and their way of life had been a matter of common family descent, but now the "covenant" with the invisible God made these a matter of law (Ex. 24.8; 34.10). That God's choice was conscious is already apparent in the covenant with Abraham (Gen. 17.2). A covenant requires a certain "parity" between those who contract it: precisely this quality of parity characterizes Abraham's consciousness.

Abraham's propensity, which reappeared in Isaac and Jacob as an independent quest for knowledge of God — the capacity to cognize the essence of the invisible God more and more

THE CHURCH

in his different aspects—culminates powerfully in Moses. Through him, a people become *the* people. One could say that such nearness to God was never again reached in the history of the Hebrews—certainly never by the rulers and leaders of the people. In the Prophets the idea of the Messiah ripens and with it the idea of the coming age, when every human being will be "chosen" and rich in divine knowledge. To reach this state one must first pass through the stage of being "a child of God." Those who do not draw their deeds and knowledge from the folk-soul as "children of Abraham," but who sacrifice their individual being are called the children of God. They "are born not of blood, nor of the will of the flesh, nor of the will of man" (John 1.13), but live and act directly out of the divine which permeates them. These men become the heralds of the Logos-Light.

A further step, a new turning-point—recorded in St. John's Gospel—occurs with the incarnation of the Logos. It becomes possible to behold his radiance. At first the attainment of this stage is restricted to a few, the closest circle of disciples, including John the Evangelist himself. But we can always hope and strive so that later several, many, including "we" ourselves, may also reach this stage: "Beloved, now are we the sons of God, and it doth not yet appear what we shall be: but we know that, when he shall appear, we shall be like him; for we shall see him as he is" (1.John 3.2). This is seeing God face to face (1.Cor. 13.12; 2.Cor. 4.6; Ezekiel 39.23,29). St. John too refers to this same stage, when he speaks about the radiance—glory—(John 17.24), or when he says: "And we have seen his glory (*dóxa*)" (John 1.14). To be a child of God is not the final stage, but only the starting-point for the Christian development of consciousness. Children of God are those who "essence" directly out of God, who are "led by the Spirit of God" (Romans 8.14). This starting-point is not simply given, but is a spiritual disposition, which must be earned through great effort. For instance, human beings today may work toward it by means of the Rosicrucian meditation *Ex Deo nascimur* — "Out of God are we born." Here nothing is given, no facts are stated. Only in and through the meditation is its content to be realized. And, unless its content is made real, any meditation, however worthy and necessary remains at best a striving. The saying "I am the way, the truth, and the life: no man cometh unto the Father, but by me" (John 14.6) is also appropriate for contemporary humanity. The first phrase of the Rosicrucian meditation — *Ex Deo nascimur* — includes therefore, if thoroughly meditated, the following sentences: *In Christo morimur — Per Spiritum Sanctum reviviscimus*. "In Christ we die" — "Through the Holy Spirit we are born again." Only in this way can we become aware of God the Father. When being a child of God was still possible without meditation, one could still perceive the living light of Divinity at the edge of one's experiences of consciousness, or one could have at least an inkling of it. Today man very rarely experiences his own perceiving and thinking. He usually only experiences their results and therefore finds the Divine neither in nature nor in "cognition."

When the spirit dwells in the individual, he then becomes "all-knowing" (1.John 2.27) like Heraclitus who thought that he was capable of cognizing everything, not actually but potentially. This is a step beyond being a child of God.

The Rosicrucian meditation points the way from being a child of God to being quickened by the Spirit. In its formulation — all three sentences are in the plural — the meditation shows the supraindividual, pan-human aspect of the path, prophetically indicated in the New Testament (also by use of the plural): "For where two or three are gathered together in my name..." (Matt. 18.20); "*Our* Father..."; "and *we* have seen His glory..." (John 1.14); "And when the day of Pentecost was fully come, they were all with one accord in one place" (Acts 2.1).

"What is more edifying than light?"—"Conversation," comes the answer in Goethe's fairy tale. But this is true only of certain special conversations which, aiming beyond words at word-less understanding, rest on such an understanding or "harmony" in the sphere beyond words. Since man is a Logos-being, he can radiate the light of the Word. But the Word requires at least two people. Only in this way does the human word, even the unspoken word, encounter the human understanding and shine back. *That* is the Logos-being's presence on earth, his being-with-men, until the end of the aeon. In this shining back and forth, a spiritual reality is built up: the name of the I am, who receives His earthly and cosmic reality through human deeds of cognition and love (Matt. 25.40-45).[44] The relation of the Logos-being to man is one of reciprocal indwelling—this is what makes a human being human—but the Logos-being can have its earthly realization only in humanity, in the common reality of *all* human beings. For the Logos is present in everyone, and man cannot find his own reality alone, but only in the totality of the Logos-Light. The Logos-nature cannot unfold in isolation, in single human beings.

The inter-human reality which seeks its incarnation in human beings and in humanity as a whole is called the *church*, whose true reality is the invisible human community neither built by hands, nor organized and institutionalized. It should be the task of every *visible* church to lead to this invisible church, to the "people" of the spirit. What is really individual in man is not his feeling being, nor his will-life. If he orients himself by these, he becomes more and more a collective being, basically connected with his fellow-men through common interests, instincts and passions, but at the same time separated from his fellow-men by these very aspects which make him fight against them. It is not the shadowy aspects of his light-nature that constitute man's individuality, but what he adds to the light-being, what can grow out of itself according to the characteristic quality of the Logos. This is the meaning of the parable of the talents (Matt. 25.14-30), as of the passage: "For whosoever hath, to him shall be given, and he shall have more abundance: but whosoever hath not, from him shall be taken away even that he hath" (Matt. 13.12; Mark 4.25; Luke 8.18,19,26).

The Word cannot be preserved or stored unchanged, it either grows or it perishes. That he can add to what has been given to him is the truly individual aspect of man. But this is paradoxical, since light and Logos are the common element and cannot even be imagined as one's "personal being" or "personal property."

Instead of a "lineage" — even a spiritual one — like "children of Abraham," or "children of God," a new image arises for the relation between human beings: they are still children of God, but now, in harmony with this, emphasis is placed on "neighborliness." They are to become brothers, brothers of Christ. *This*, rather than common descent, has to determine their relation to each other. The "memory," the continuing effectiveness of the force of *common* spiritual descent, is extinguished with the death on the cross, but through this experience individual resurrection can occur in the spirit which can experience this dying. This is the meaning of the event of Pentecost. But for this to come about, men must be "*homothymadón*" — of one mind, together.[45]

It is obvious that difficult obstacles have to be overcome in order to realize this "*homothymadón.*" These obstacles lie in man himself and not without good reason. Man needs a "house." This has been given to him in the form of a living physical body with which the psycho-spiritual aspect identifies itself in part. Unless the psycho-spiritual is connected to its house, it cannot cognize, as is the case during sleep. What man usually designates with the word "I" does *not* cause him to fall asleep or to awake. But since the I reappears on awakening, it must have existed, independently of the living body, during sleep. In cognition, too, the I must become independent of the body,[46] otherwise it would not be true cognition but merely a natural process. In the house of the physical body the psycho-spiritual part of man gradually learns to become independent. Thereby it can later "remain" conscious, living in "finer" houses, physically unconfined, in the "living temple" (1.Peter 2.5), which is a building free of minerality.

With the fall there occurred a partial identification of soul and spirit with the physical body. Sleep and death save man from entering this identity completely. Nevertheless, through the "fall" into corporeality, in which dream-like perception of the sphere of life was lost, the human sensitive powers change. In their origin these powers are powers of pure light, created for the cognition of the world. Through them the world becomes reality: its forms and reality persist in this light. Since, like all living things, the living body has a form, life itself had to assume a particular form and the living idea began to work in the body, which is filled with what is mineral. But only when the body disintegrates does the "mineral" really come into being. In order to move and sustain itself, the living form must find a corresponding form of sensitivity. This may be seen in reflex movements, in the capacity for movement itself, and in the desires and appetites of the body in which the soul does not take part, as, for example, in the feeling of hunger or thirst. In man, however, sensitivity remained predominantly formless, ready to adopt any form for cognition. Cognition always requires a partial transformation into what is to be cognized.[47] This transformation takes place in the true I, in the sensitive powers and in the living man. But man does not follow it consciously. Relying on the immutably physical, he does not experience the transformation, but only what is already cognized. Sensitivity was originally directed at the world; but with the *fall*, the emanating powers of sensitivity or feeling, which were originally intended to serve the processes of cognition, were largely turned back onto the I. In this way the powers of transformation, of identity with the world, became ego powers — i.e. powers of identity with oneself, of self-feeling, and the wish to experience oneself — and were withdrawn from the process of cognition. As a result of this "reversal," new forms of subjective, personal sensitivity arose from these radiant powers. In "self-feeling," something of the essence of the I, which is a self-experiencing, self-cognizing light, appears on a lower level. Sensitivity was originally *light*. Through the fall, a process which still continues today, the powers of sensitivity become powers of self-feeling, that imitate the gesture of the I without becoming cognition. The urge toward self-feeling creates a closed soul, which defends its boundaries and leads an autonomous life. This soul, indeed, consists of its boundaries and their protection, becoming an ensouled form of sensitivity, made up of interlinked closures, patterns of reaction and association—"complexes"—whose formative character and "independent" behavior are described in depth by psychology. These forms have more or less fallen away from the dominion of the I. They have a certain autonomy: i.e. the soul can revolt against its "master," the I. It can also crowd its "master" completely out of the field of vision, giving rise in this way to an I-less existence, which does not behold itself. This means a restless being, driven by desires—a being who, in endless longing, has desires only for their own sake.

All these "forms" of life and sensitivity are closures, "*gestalts*." Traditionally called "houses" or "dwellings," they are inhabited by demons or impure spirits, though contemporary psychology gives them more impersonal names. The essence of these spirits is that they have a definite form—a form of reaction, of fear etc.—over which the subject has no power. One can fight these "inhabitants" and drive them out; but if their "dwelling," the enduring habit of the soul, is not dissolved, they often return "multiplied" (Matt. 12.43-45; Luke 11.24-26). St. Paul, too, writes of this psychic life which has wrongly become independent (Romans 7.15-23).

Sensitivity should really be less "awake" than it is. The I should be awake, and the powers of sensitivity should mediate sensations—even on the spiritual plane—to the I. Schooling in perfect cognition proceeds by the dissolution of psychic habits. Thereby the life of the soul is quieted and the emotions that circle endlessly within themselves are overcome. The Buddhist Eightfold Path consists of such "form-dissolving" exercises.[48]

BECOMING AWARE OF THE LOGOS

In earlier times human soul-life was guided by the gods, as representatives of the I-Being who was to come later. These gods were the real subject of the "experiences" mediated by the sensitivity. Hence the small child today still says in an all-embracing fashion "mother," "milk," "world," and not "mother *is*...," "world *is*...," etc. The child is still identical, in the *pure* light of sensitivity, with what it "experiences." If the connection with God, which initially stood for the I, is lost, and if the I does not enter its domain—or enters only weakly—the certainty which is the foundation of life disappears. "Rootless" souls arise, in which something soul-like with its own form of sensitivity gains the upper hand. When fundamental certainty is missing, fear arises; and where there is fear, aggressiveness, hatred and cruelty take root. Cain's gesture is enacted in the outer world. Worldviews appear which are the opponents of love, because they consider love as a weakness. Thus honest thinkers discover that fear is contemporary man's central, if hidden, experience.

In the New Testament the psychic sphere of "impure spirits" is described in depth. In his First Epistle St. John emphasizes the dissolution of psychic forms as a path to inner righteousness. He also speaks of fear: "There is no fear in love; but perfect love casteth out fear: because fear hath mutilation. He that feareth is not made perfect in love" (1.John 4.18).[49] Mutilation means that we are hindered from complete surrender and devotion to the other by attachment to "self-being" and forms of undissolved sensitivity. These are forms of sensitivity, which no longer feel the other person or the other thing. By means of them one becomes on the contrary egotistically "sensitive" to oneself and insensitive to the other. Fear means egoity, fear for one-

THE CHURCH

self; as long as there is fear, there is no true, complete love. Man brings a partial consciousness out of his past. At first consciousness sees only partially; it consists of sections, snippets, which contradict each other; and the soul is restless because the parts, the psychic forms, fight each other. Man knows "in part"; the world is patchwork to him. Peace, "not as the world giveth" (John 14.27), means the harmonizing of this divided being—the Buddha's inner oceanic quiet—by which man is freed from reacting and becomes a true I-Being. This development is a deed, it does not happen by itself. The psychic, what St. Paul calls "the natural," must transform itself into spirit. In his consciousness-soul man can look on his past consciousness, on what he has already thought. His "natural" development has led him to this point. But the consciousness-soul is a transitional stage. It cannot last. Either man will fall back into the attitude of the intellectual soul, which uses cognitive powers without being aware of them; or he will develop into the spirit-self, which experiences itself as a spiritual being, without the need to rely upon the past, the "outer," and which lives in the present, realizing the present in its experience of it. Out of this present the new human community can be formed.[50]

In earlier times man experienced himself as a member of a community. Later on, participation in the life of the community became more and more ritualized—there were times when one had to go to the temple. Thereby cultural life was separated from everyday life, and likewise from cognition. In modern times, with the Reformation, human beings began to make decisions on the basis of individual conscience.

Today many people lack the traditional possibility of religious experience and so also lack the experience of community. For them there is no church that is finished and built once and for all. This possibility is foreseen in the New Testament: "But thou, when thou prayest, enter into thy closet, and when thou hast shut thy door, pray to thy Father which is in secret; and thy Father which seeth in secret shall reward thee openly" (Matt. 6.6); ". . . the hour cometh, when ye shall neither in this mountain, nor yet at Jerusalem, worship the Father . . . But the hour cometh, and now is, when the true—*alethinoí*—worshippers shall worship the Father in spirit and in truth—*alétheia*—for the Father seeketh such to worship him. God is spirit: and they that worship him must worship him in spirit and in truth" (John 4.21-24). Out of those who pray in solitude a community of the spirit can be formed. For the spirit is the common element of all human beings. The formation of community is only possible, however, when a "house," a dwelling for a being, is established. In earlier times the impulse for the formation of a community was given by a higher being; today this must proceed from human beings.

Every idea and all understanding has its origin in the intuitive sphere which is common to all mankind. Truth and cognition would not be possible otherwise. A truth would be true only "for me" or for a limited number of people— and that would not be truth at all. A language is valid for a particular group of people, but it cannot belong to a single individual. An historical impulse, as for example the Baroque, marks every aspect of the life of an age with a uniform style. Such realities do not originate in the individual, but are impulses of an ideal nature; they are "ideas" of superhuman dimensions. A language with all its characteristic properties, its immanent wisdom, its "philosophy," is not created by men, but by superhuman beings. To be able to think this means that one can form ideas for oneself about

THE CHURCH

higher beings who can "think" a language, a period style, or even the entire cognitive capacity of humanity. Behind all language stands the language of mankind, whose "thinker" is the Logos.

Many intuitions await their "incarnation" through man. They are not "finished" in an earthly sense, but receive their earthly form through man. Man is able to remove the obstacles to intuition. It is his work "to prepare the way" (Isaiah 40.3). When this work is done, the intuition appears on earth.

There are intuitions — like a language, like thinking — for which one human being is not sufficient. In earlier times communities formed themselves through just such intuitions. In more recent times a receptive house must first exist in the form of human groups. If this condition is fulfilled, the intuition enters as a being into the prepared house. In the Apocalypse such a living intuition is called the "angel of the church," and the earthly representative, whom he inspires, is called the leader of the community. The angel of the church is already active in each individual during the building of the house. The community is the intuition of the being in each person. If the human community disintegrates, the "angel" withdraws. Such a being is part of every human association which is a true community and not just an externally organized group.

In this community individuality is not given up, because it freely gives itself up. Surrender strengthens the community's existence as it strengthens the existence of the beings of the angelic hierarchies. "In my Father's house are many mansions" (John 14.2). Once the obstacles are overcome, they serve to make possible the very unity, whose archetypal image is the union of the Father with the Son: "... keep through thine own name those whom thou hast given me, that they may be one, as we are" (John 17.11); "That they all may be one; as thou, Father, art in me, and I in thee" (John 17.21).

One person is not enough to form an invisible church whose head is the Logos. St. Matthew describes the earthly beginning of this Church when he writes: "Amen I say unto you, that if two of you shall agree on earth as touching any thing that they shall ask, it shall be done for them of my Father which is in heaven. For where two or three are gathered together in my name, there am I in the midst of them" (Matt. 18.19-20).

One human being alone, in his activity on behalf of others, cannot stand against the evil on earth, because he cannot realize his humanity, his Logos-being, by himself.

The Messiah has come and is with human beings: "And behold, I am with you every day until the end of the aeon" (Matt. 28.20). One may ask, what does "every day" mean in relation to "until the fulfilment of the aeon?" The answer follows from experience. The statement does not indicate a finished state, but something to be realized by us from day to day: namely, spiritual communion with the spirit of humanity — who seeks to incarnate in the invisible church which is the real life of humanity — the spirit of humanity, from whom all intuitions for the further life of our endangered earth can come.

TEN

Cháris and Alétheia

Two ideas, two words — *cháris* and *alétheia* — are introduced at the beginning of St. John's Gospel in close connection with each other. Translated as "grace" and "truth," it is obvious that these words are empty phrases for modern man, and that theology and philosophy misunderstand them. Theology understands grace as something that comes to a person without his earning it, while philosophy (and natural science likewise) understands truth as the coincidence of thinking or representation with reality (or the perceived facts.) And if reality — how one acts — corresponds with one's thinking or mental picture, then there results what is called "ethical truth." Going even further, philosophy sometimes relativizes truth, and thereby ultimately denies it. But if we are "comparing" truth, if we wish to test its "correctness," then the question immediately arises: How do I know "reality," with which I am supposedly drawing a comparison? Since there is no answer to this question (for cognition of "reality" would be truth itself, and there would be nothing to compare it with), it is clear that the idea of truth has been lost. This confusion of truth with correctness has arisen both from naive realism's premise that "reality" can exist without my cognizing it, and that nevertheless I can know it, and the Church's traditional teaching that a Revelation can exist without the possibility or necessity of a human being to cognize it. Those who think in this way always forget that they are giving detailed information about a non-cognized reality, which they are thereby claiming paradoxically to know, whether it is a material reality or the content of Revelation.

The results of misunderstanding "grace," on the other hand, are fatalism, the doctrine of predestination and, ultimately, absolute determinism, which excludes all possibility of freedom.

Both of these, the view that reality cannot be known (agnosticism) and the view that freedom is impossible, are in contradiction to the text and spirit of St. John and the whole New Testament. Not only is every truth, at least potentially accessible to man (John 16.13), but the depths of the Godhead are also accessible to him (1.Cor. 2.10). At the same time the Son makes man free (John 8.32,36).

To understand the words *alétheia* and *cháris* we must become aware of the fact that both concepts are related to inner human experiences. *Alétheia* is the negation of *létheia*, which derives from the verb *lanthánein*, to hide, to be hidden, to forget. After death, the one who has died drinks "forgetting" from the river *Léthe* in the Greek underworld. In early Greek times, *alétheia* was already understood as "unhiddenness," and this is in fact a more dynamic concept of truth than the concept of truth as some fixed, permanently valid "correctness." One can penetrate unhiddenness forever, from sheath to sheath. Truth as "unhiddenness" is never finite, nor is it independent of cognition. In this sense, truth is always "revelation" of what was previously hidden. It emerges from "oblivion." The "original," "natural" condition would be one in which everything was cognized in a light-filled world. But this condition was lost—*lanthánein* has this meaning too—in *létheia*. Man had to pass through forgetting, darkness, the unrevealed, in order that *he* might *become* the cognizer.

It is characteristic of today's reflected consciousness that it awakens only through its own past. It sees only finished, fixed forms, constructs, facts, and does not notice how they appear and enter into consciousness. Thinking, perceiving and mental picturing (representing) are not experienced as processes. They remain in the background, "hidden" and "forgotten." The world's living, active sphere is neither perceived nor included in reality. Therefore the world seems to consist of the finished contents of consciousness—the past of living present-consciousness. Man is attached to this past, because he feels himself, his own existence through it. This past is so foreign to and different from himself as a living cognizer that in the beginning man can experience himself only through it. As long as the cognizer does not discover this situation he is living a contradiction. He can only recognize the past as reality, and therefore he tries to find his own reality in the world of the past. "Man is nothing but...," followed by something which is not man at all. "Thinking is nothing but...," "The I is nothing but...," followed by something which is not thinking, not I, but physics, chemistry, biology, cybernetics, or "spirit," "soul," "divinity" etc., all things which the reflected consciousness thinks or imagines.

Consciousness' self-denial, by which it tries to derive itself from what is not conscious (which is nevertheless its content), and by means of which it attempts to explain cognition through what has been cognized (and only "cognized" through cognition), demonstrates the most serious disease of human consciousness, *létheia*, or forgetting: the forgetting of the *process* of thinking and cognizing, which cannot be experienced by ordinary consciousness but only logically deduced, because the contents of consciousness vary, change and multiply, and so point to something in process, to an event which must originate in something that is active in the present, something living.

Truth as unhiddenness means that it is possible to develop the faculty of cognition further. The first step to a qualitative, further development of consciousness is the formation of a consciousness of the present, in which one no longer needs to rely on the contents of the past in order to stay awake, but can say, out of the experience of the present, I am.

In this way one attains the sphere of life mentioned in Chapter 6 which St. Paul calls "the first heaven." The ability to perceive the present, to perceive the life of the world and of consciousness simultaneously, to experience its transparence and transillumination—this unhidden and unforgotten state of life is called *alétheia* by St. John and signifies the attainment of the spiritual self in man. It is the light that bears witness of itself, as described in Chapter 4. *Alétheia*, as an experience of consciousness, goes beyond individual, earthly life. It could be said of one who stands in *alétheia* that he is true, is *alethés*, that "he is truth itself." One has *alétheia*, is truth, as long as one does not lose one's consciousness or "fall asleep." When all reflected consciousness disappears, when all representations and memories pass away, in life as after death, one does not drink of "oblivion" from the stream of *léthe*. Understood thus, *alétheia* is continuity of the light in consciousness.

In his Prologue St. John describes the only-begotten Son

as "full of *cháris* and *alétheia*" (John 1.14); later he says: "For the law was given by Moses, but grace and truth came by Jesus Christ" (John 1.17). The word "came" — *egéneto* — implies that these realities did not exist from eternity, but are *earthly* realities. Since the incarnation, and through the one who incarnated, these realities are attainable by men only on the earth. As an idea, *alétheia* must be conceived of in such a way that the expression "doing the truth" becomes meaningful (John 3.21; 1.John 1.6). "To worship the Father in spirit and in truth" (John 4.23-24) characterizes the quality of *alétheia* as we are trying to understand it. Also: "And ye shall know the truth and the truth shall make you free" (John 8.32). "I am the way and the truth" (John 14.6). This means that the I am is *alétheia*, that the true I begins where the I am rests within itself, without proof, without support. All proofs and supports are only for the I; and only through the I do they find their power of existence. The "spirit of truth" (John 14.17; 16.13) is the Holy Spirit, who guides man to all truth (John 14.17; 16.13). This is the spirit which is common to all men and is attained at the stage of the spirit-self. "To sanctify through the truth" (John 17.17-19) means that human beings become "holy," entirely and truly human, only in the sphere of life, in the present, and not in the world of the past, "this world," which they must "conquer" and overcome. When one is of the truth (John 18.37; 1.John 3.19), one hears the voice of the Logos-being. "No lie is of the truth" (1.John 2.21). If one understands "truth" here in its ordinary, unenlightened sense, then the Apostle's saying is very trivial. In reality it means that a lie — characterized in the following verse — does not derive from the stage of consciousness of *alétheia*.

"For this cause came I unto the world, that I should bear

witness unto the truth; every one that is of the truth heareth my voice" (John 18.37). Following this, Pilate poses his question, "What is truth?" Humanity does not understand the word, because it is not of the truth. But the truth can remain; it can "dwell" in man (2.John 2). This is the stage of consciousness called *alétheia*. That truth is in a human being (John 8.44; 1.John 1.8; 2.4), has the same meaning. It means a mutual abiding. A human being can be of the truth and the truth can be in him: he can walk in the truth (3.John 3,4).

The adjectives *alethés* and *alethinós* are used in the same sense as *alétheia* to mean truthful, true, as in the stage of consciousness described above: true meat, true drink (John 6.55); the true light, light that experiences itself; the light of the world (John 1.9), the true bread (John 6.32); the true judgment (John 8.16); the true vine (John 15.1); the true God (John 17.3; 1.John 5.20; 1.Thess. 1.9); the true tabernacle (Hebr. 8.2). A thing, a person, or an action, as for example "witnessing" is true and truthful if, during its experience, consciousness is not interrupted, as is the case in ordinary thinking. Ordinary thinking does not experience its own source. Its rising and flowing is continuously interrupted. When consciousness experiences itself in its activity, when it looks through its own activity, that is called *alethés*, *alethinós*.

One who walks in the truth can say, without reservation, I am. He says it wordlessly, for the sphere of truth is the sphere of wordless thinking.[51] The I am is *alétheia*; truth is *cognized* truth. The Word, the Logos, belongs to it. Words are without meaning for it. The I am engenders the truth for me and for you. The truth is equivalent to the understanding that lives between two or three human beings; it is equivalent to the unconcealment, the overcoming of concealment: it is being present, presentness. The possibility of presentness originates in the Word, the Logos.

Truth is not correctness, the correspondence of representation or law with being, but it is the correspondence of the statement, proposition or action with its content. There are statements which confirm themselves — for example, "I am" — and there are assertions, like "I am not" or "you are not," which negate themselves. Despite this, out of contemporary habits of thought, one hears it repeatedly said, "Thinking is not . . . ," "Thinking is nothing but . . . ," "The I does not exist . . . ," "Man does not exist. . . ." Truth consists in the correspondence of the asserting as such with the assertion. The statement "I am lying" is as impossible as the statements "truth is not," "cognizing is not." Unconcealment, "un-oblivion" means that one does not allow the act of speaking to be concealed or forgotten behind what is spoken.

John condenses his message in the formula: "The spirit is truth" (1.John 5.6). The spirit in man leads to all truths. With the appearance of the Logos-being on earth, "in this world," the revelation to mankind begins. In earlier times revelation was possible only for a few chosen people through the dimming down and giving up of the I am. Then, it was said "I, Osiris," "I, Anu." Now, the Son is the revealer of the Father; everything that was hidden before — the "mystery" — begins to appear in the open through him. Paul writes of the revelation through the Logos of the secret (*mysterion*) "which was kept secret since the world began" (Romans 16.25): "But we speak about the wisdom of God — *theoû sofía* — which is concealed in the mystery — *en misterio* — which God ordained before aeons, but revealed unto us through the spirit" (1.Cor. 2.7,10). In Colossians (Col. 1.26)

131

and Ephesians (Eph. 3.4) he writes about this mystery in a similar manner. In this way *alétheia* attains human and cosmic measure. The appearance of the Logos, the in-dwelling of the spirit in man, brings about cosmic unconcealment. The potentially uninterrupted working of the Logos in the world and in human consciousness is revealed in transparent clarity. "No man has seen God at any time; the only-begotten Son, which is in the bosom of the Father, he hath declared him" (literally: he has lived Him as an example) (John 1.18).[52] The God who is present in every man has brought the Son into earthly visibility, into unconcealment. This is what is meant by seeing "face to face." One may therefore say, on the basis of the New Testament, that, with regard to human cognition, Christianity is a permanent striving, indeed a struggle, to achieve this seeing "face to face." This seeing transforms the human being into a likeness with what is seen so that he becomes not only the likeness but also the image of God: "But the Lord is the Spirit: and where the Spirit of the Lord is, there is freedom. But we all, with open face beholding as in a glass the glory of the Lord, are metamorphosed into the same image from glory into glory, (even as) by the spirit of the Lord" (2.Cor. 3.18). "For God, who commanded the light to shine out of darkness, hath shined in our hearts, to give the light of the knowledge of the glory of God in the face of Jesus Christ" (2.Cor. 4.6). This recalls the previously quoted passage: ". . . for we shall see him, as he is" (1.John 3.2). What, earlier, was only seen by the angels of the little ones (Matt. 18.10), becomes attainable on earth for men — a possibility, already foreseen by Ezekiel (Ez. 39.29).[53]

Christianity's sole object, its entire striving, stands under the sign of *alétheia*, unconcealment. What was earlier practiced as divine wisdom concealed in the mystery schools, becomes public, becomes—potentially—the common good of all humanity. It enters the light—indeed, *is* the light. Here, simply, is the decisive motive of the leaders of the Jews, the reason why they wanted to get the Logos-bearer out of the way (John 11.47).

The world of *alétheia* begins as the Age of the Spirit. Nothing remains hidden any longer. Everything is given to man, including the ultimate meaning, the final possibility of the destiny of humanity and the earth. From now on, the Godhead can work only through man. At the same time, however, man is supposed to realize *alétheia* as a state of consciousness. If he does not, the possibility of understanding all living relationships, the possibility of freedom and love, is turned into its opposite: chaos, unfreedom and the war of all against all.

Unconcealment entered the world in that the Word became flesh. Consequently, one can behold the word, which until then could not be used freely. Seeing the word means freedom from the word, freedom in the word, because one stands before it. That this potentiality has remained concealed until today is what is un-Christian about our culture.

The Logos-being brings two new possibilities to humanity: *alétheia* and *cháris*. In the New Testament these two ideas appear in connection with each other not only in St. John's Gospel, but also in his Second Epistle (2.John 2.3) and, most significantly, in St. Paul's Epistle to the Colossians: "For the hope which is laid up for you in heaven, whereof you heard before in the Logos of the *alétheia* of the gospel; which is come unto you, as it is in all the world; and bringeth forth fruit as it doth also in you since the day ye heard of it, and knew the *cháris* of God in *alétheia*" (Col 1.5, 6).

BECOMING AWARE OF THE LOGOS

Cháris is known in or through *alétheia*. Through the incarnation of the Logos, *cháris* and *alétheia* came into the world (John 1.14,17). But these gifts are not unilaterally "given," for, to receive them, the human gesture of receiving is required. The verb which expresses this, *lambánein* means both "receiving" and "taking." It is also used in conjunction with prepositions, as in "*katalambánein*" or "*paralambánein*." *Lambánein* appears three times in the Prologue to St. John's Gospel, and it appears a fourth time in verse 16 (John 1.5,11, 12,16). *Lambánein* is here neither mere receiving nor mere taking, as it is on other occasions in the New Testament. Neither *alétheia* nor *cháris* are meant to be gifts, for on the one hand they are aspects of the world, world-realities, while on the other they are human abilities, which are not granted but have to be earned.

The word *aléthia* appears with greater frequency in St. John's Gospel than in the other Gospels. The word *cháris*, on the other hand, appears only three times in the Prologue and the immediately following verses. In its place the word *agápe* — love — and its corresponding verbal form predominates. We also find the word *cháris* in St. Luke's Gospel and in Acts (which he wrote). Both words — *alétheia* and *cháris* — are often used in the Pauline Epistles, while in St. Luke (4.22) and Acts (14.3; 20.32) we find the expression: "The Logos of *cháris*" of "The word of grace." In St. Luke the subject is Jesus' first teaching "in the power of the Spirit" (Luke 4.14): "And all bare him witness, and wondered at the gracious words — lit., the words of *cháris* — which proceeded out of his mouth" (Luke 4.22). The translation "gracious words" show that the meaning was not understood. "Words of *cháris*" signifies discourse that has the power to convince, so that the listeners bear witness to him. The

134

CHÁRIS AND ALÉTHEIA

astonishment caused by this kind of teaching is often described: "And they were astonished at his doctrine: for his word—logos—was with power—*exousía*" (Luke 4.32). And a few verses later: "What a word is this! For with authority and power—*dýnamai*—he commanded the unclean spirits, and they come out" (Luke 4.36). St. Matthew writes: "For he taught them as one having authority—*exousía*—and not as the scribes" (Matt. 7.29). St. Mark says the same, and adds: "What thing is this? A new doctrine out of power (*exousía*)" (Mark 1.27). The astonishment is described by St. Matthew and St. Mark (Matt. 22.33; Mark 11.18), while in St. John the servants of the Pharisees say: "Never man spake like this man" (John 7.46). ("Speaking" here is *laleîn*, which has been discussed in Chapter 5.) The word of grace —*cháris*—has power: it works so that it is understood directly—intuitively—as a child understands words when it learns to speak. This word has power over "unclean spirits"; it has power to bring about "signs and miracles": "In this manner they had spent some time in freedom, teaching about the Lord, who gave his word of grace and made signs and miracles through their hands" (Acts 14.3) The "word of *cháris*" is always a *doing*.

St. Luke informs us about the specific quality of this "doing" in another passage: "For if ye love them which love you, what *cháris* have ye? for sinners also love those that love them. And if ye do good to them which do good to you, what *cháris* have ye? for sinners also do even the same. And if ye lend to them of whom ye hope to receive, what *cháris* have ye? for sinners also lend to sinners, to receive as much again" (Luke 6. 32-34). In the King James Version, *cháris* is translated by the word "thank," which makes no sense, although *cháris* does mean "thank"; but it also means everything which gives joy: "gracefulness, charm," "mercy," "favor," "grace," "goodwill," "kindness," and what these call forth in response, "acknowledgement," "appreciation," "thankfulness." What is common to all these is that they indicate something "beyond" the necessary, "beyond" what was asked for, something "gratis," free of charge, as is suggested in the above passage. This must therefore be understood as follows: one who does something only for the return, or on the speculation thereof, what kind of *cháris* has he? The teaching of *cháris* has to do more with giving than with taking. The passage therefore concludes: "But love ye your enemies, and do good, and lend, hoping for nothing again . . ." (Luke 6.35).

Before this, however, it says: "And as ye would that men should do to you, do ye also to them likewise" (Luke 6.31). This means: Don't wait until the other begins, *you* begin first. To do good in abundance, beyond one's duties, is *cháris*. "Doth he thank the servant because he did the things that were commanded him? I trow not. So likewise ye, when ye shall have done all those things which are commanded you, say, We are unprofitable servants, we have done that which was our duty to do" (Luke 17.9-10). The word "unprofitable" means not to bring any benefit, to bring nothing "beyond" or "more." "Give, and it shall be given unto you; good measure, pressed down, and shaken together, and running over, shall men give into your bosom. For with the same measure that ye mete withal it shall be measured to you again" (Luke 6.38). A generous, rich abundance must enter into a man's heart, so that he may become one who gives instead of remaining one who takes.

The useless servant is mentioned in another parable, dealing with the talents which the Lord entrusts to his servants

(Luke 19.12-17); Matt. 25.14-30). Those who earned more are rewarded. From one who merely returns what he has received even that is taken away and given to the one who has most: "For unto every one that hath shall be given, and he shall have abundance: but from him that hath not shall be taken away even that which he hath. And cast ye the unprofitable servant into outer darkness: there shall be weeping and gnashing of teeth" (Matt. 25.29-30). The inner law of these gifts, these abilities or potentialities, is that they either grow or perish, bringing the "unprofitable" owner into perdition. "And the Logos of God increased..." "And Stephen, full of *cháris* and might — *dýnamis* — did great wonders and miracles among the people" (Acts 6.7-6; 12.24; 19.20). "For whosoever hath, to him shall be given, and he shall have more *abundance*; but whosoever hath not, from him shall be taken away even that which he hath" (Matt. 13.12; Luke 8.18). Thus the secret of the Logos in man is described. "Growing," "increasing" is the fundamental quality of this Logos. "For the soul has the Logos, which grows out of itself," as Heraclitus says. "He must increase, I must decrease," says John the Baptist. "And the Word, the Logos of God increased..." (Acts 6.7; 12.24; 19.20) "Increasing" is always (already in Heraclitus) expressed by the word *auxánein*. Thus this "growing" is, from the beginning, and correctly, related to the process of cognition.

Contemplating the *cháris*-idea reveals that a similar "beyond" or "more" can also be applied to the moral sphere, and that precisely this "more" characterizes the new morality in contrast to the old one. Thus, too, the new commandment is distinguished from the old. The old commandment, "Thou shalt love thy neighbour as thyself" (Lev. 19.18) does not imply a "comparison"; but rather means: Love

137

your neighbor because, in reality, he is *you*, he bears your true being and, only in loving him does your true being therefore come to life. The new commandment is: "A new commandment give I unto you, that ye love one another; as I have loved you, that ye also love one another" (John 13.14; 15.12). The difference between the new commandment and the old commandment (which does not become obsolete through the new) lies in the speaker. The I am does not give humanity his love under the above-mentioned conditions. He does not teach "Love thy neighbor as thyself" because his being, despite everything that he encounters among the disciples, i.e. the desertion or the betrayal, does not only come into life in the other, but is given freely by him in the greatest possible abundance. The I am's love does not "consider," it is unconditional and serves. *Serving* is the other formulation of the new commandment. It is contrasted with the ambition of the disciples: "Ye know that the princes of the Gentiles exercise dominion over them, and they that are great exercise authority upon them. But it shall not be so among you: but whosoever will be chief among you, let him be your servant: "Even as the Son of man came not to be ministered unto, but to minister and to give his life — *psyché* — a ransom for many" (Matt. 20.25-28); also Matt. 23.11; Mark 10.42-44; 9.35; Luke 22.25-27). The washing of the feet (John 13.4-10) exemplifies this service. "If ye know these things, happy are ye if ye do them" (John 13.17). The "more," "profit" or "abundance" is elaborated in the Sermon on the Mount (Matt. 5.39-48) and in the Sermon in the Plain (Luke 6.27-35), but St. John gives it a direct formulation.

From these statements it is clear that both realities, *cháris* and *alétheia*, indicate and presuppose the capacity for beginning, for first or primal beginning. Truth — cognition — cannot arise from conditions or causes. Truth must arise freely, i.e. out of primal beginning, without a *because* or *what for*. In the sphere of action, the deeds of *cháris* are deeds of love, of unconditioned intuition, or in spiritual science, "moral intuition." Creation out of nothing is the ability, the reality which John calls *arché*, or primal beginning. In creation, *cháris* and *alétheia*, love and cognition are *one*. Out of love for that which is not yet, something *becomes* cognized and so it *becomes*: something new.

Alétheia enables me to find and to utter the truth out of myself, proceeding "from unconcealment to unconcealment." *Cháris* enables me to practice "grace" out of grace. Both realities reflect and ray out. They cannot be owned; they only exist in giving and taking. "Grace for grace" it says in St. John's Gospel (John 1.16).

Cháris, *alétheia* and "this world" designate the three planes of reality.

"This world" is the past, the world as it appears in mirrored consciousness, the world of things and of facts.

Alétheia is the living presence, the processes of light, of cognition, of the world's becoming. It is the world of living cognizing.

Cháris, from the point of view of mirrored consciousness, is the future world, which is not yet present, but for which we can sow seeds out of *cháris*. It is the mightiest, seminal reality. Reality fades from the future, through the present, into the past — the world of death, in which we live in a continuous, but rarely experienced, contradiction.

When one learns to renounce reflected, mirrored consciousness, one enters the world of *alétheia*, the world of life. "He that loveth his life — *psyché* — shall lose it; and he

BECOMING AWARE OF THE LOGOS

that hateth his life in this world shall keep it unto life eternal" (John 12.25; also Matt. 16.25 and Luke 9.24).

When one learns to renounce consciousness of the present, presence, one enters the world of *cháris*.

Renunciation is the secret of every true ascent.

That humanity can attain *alétheia* and *cháris* is the joyous message of Christianity: the kingdoms of heaven are at hand (John 1.14 and 17).

In contrast to divine world-creating love, whose human reflection, "natural love" in man, is called "first love" by John (Rev. 2.4; 1.John 4.19), earthly human love has to realize itself within the sphere of obstacles and darkness. Indeed human love needs the boundaries of the soul, its separateness, to enter the earthly world in the process of overcoming these obstacles. This is the *abundance*, which pours forth beyond the past, beyond the world which has been created so far. This abundance emerges into movement out of the I, and overcomes all calculations, every law. Spiritual cognition springs from the same source and "transforms itself, through its own essence, into love."[54]

When the spirit, the power of cognition, true to its own nature, works on earth in the "non-cognizing" world, it is love in the world of darkness, limitations, obstacles, and it overcomes all of them.[55] This is what Paul means when he speaks to the world of "knowing in part." "And now abideth faith, hope, love, these three; but the greatest of these is love" (1.Cor. 13.13).

Alétheia, or living wisdom, is the condition under which love can "remain," i.e. "abide" consciously and permanently in man — not just shine into the human life through intuition. It teaches love the "how" and is the foundation of the ability to "begin." One cannot, however, derive love from

CHÁRIS AND ALÉTHEIA

wisdom; it is always a new, further step. In the world of the I, love corresponds to wisdom. No other wisdom is of any consequence here; no other creates harmony, because no other takes into account the beginning. Love understands the beginning which cannot arise from past causes, but only from the beginning itself. In the beginning love already understands — understands "into" the future. The world of the past and the world of the present have emerged from the activity of I-beings; therefore they have laws.

Embodied wisdom is "adapation." It begins with imitation. Living being is: living word, living form, which is real only in its aliveness, not in its outer appearance which is "clothed" in the mineral. The "adaption" of the animal is inner sensitivity and activity. Man's adaptation is love, the adaptation to what, as yet, exists neither in the sphere of the soul, nor in the sphere of the living, nor in the sphere of sensitivity — an adaptation to something that is still entirely beginning.

The basis of the word, of conversation, is trust, love, for words can only in the smallest part be "explained." Without trust in the word, without the will to understand, communication is impossible. Love is the word's wing — without it, the word cannot "fly."

A single human being has no reality, the existence of "man" begins with the word that floats between I and you. The Logos connects human beings through the Word — all else is temptation or a temporary connection. To look for the connecting element elsewhere is to disregard the new commandment.

Love is above all *idea*: a light in thinking, understandable through intuition. For its realization the idea must be grasped. It must penetrate to the depths of the will, which is

141

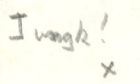

superconscious, to become therein *idea*, a new sun, a new shining day of creation, brighter than a "thousand suns" which already exist. This is the "big bang": the sun of love breaks through, bringing a new world into being.

Without the intuition of love, love cannot be understood. By explaining it through something else, even through egoity — the attempt to derive love from something else being in fact what is "good for me" — love is easily denied. The intuition of love itself *is* love: it reveals itself in it. "Being" rises in the sign of love like a new intuition, as when someone finds the "key" to playing the violin — the technique can be improved later.

"This is the redemption of man: that something in this world is done out of love. And this is redemption: That the Word became flesh."[56] Once someone has understood this existence, he knows that there can be no other human goal than the kingdom of God. It is an intuition that love is possible and that nothing else is needed.

As speaking is an interhuman reality, so too is the Logos, who speaks through human beings, and whose words do not pass away, and so, too, are the deeds men do for each other — there are no other *human* deeds — a reality rooted in the same source. To reject this reality, the reality of the Logos (Matt. 25.10), prevents it from coming into being. On earth "he" is not yet a reality, but in the sphere of life, the first heaven, he *is* reality.[57]

As the tendency of his organs to fulfill their own, individual nature is not the whole man, so also man's "self-feeling" has a partial character; it is a similar tendency for individual self-ownership. This is not man's true essence, but is man torn *out* of the world, out of being, to which he is no longer connected through his own essence.

CHÁRIS AND ALÉTHEIA

What does not serve is man's "singularity," a part which would rule in place of the whole. This is not man. What is not human in man is not in harmony with the earth. What does not surrender itself is sickness within the reality of the earth.

Salvation of the soul is possible neither for an individual nor for a couple. There is only salvation of humanity. Therefore the goal is not individual salvation, as in pre-Christian times, but the kingdom of God: true human existence, which is "at hand."

On earth we depend on material goods. Division of labor, wherein one man works for another, is therefore necessary. This should already show us that the earth is the place of the consciousness of love, of love-consciousness. Such love is not something old. Everything that preceded it was only instruction. The new love has no tradition, no ritual, no myth. It is now and always beginning. It is not "moderately balanced," not concerned about requital, and therefore it is not concerned with sex either. Sexuality is today's decadent form of the old, in-born love. It does not begin anew; it is not free. To metamorphose this, to form it humanly, is one of the greatest human tasks.

The cycle of love is: let it become, that it may *be*.

The cycle of the light is: may it experience itself.

The cycle of the past is: it is, because it is. The "why" is endless; it reaches no *beginning*. How could it — in the past?

That love might be is the earth's mission. Reciprocally, for the *earth* to be, love must also be. This means neither restoration nor restitution, but only that a first, primal beginning is possible. What is really individual is never a "renewal."

Love is not meant *for* a single human being. It rays out *from* a single human being: in order that it might be, for the sake of being. Love is being. Being takes on the form which it receives in human consciousness. For the cognizer, being is cognition; for the consciousness of love, it is love. Divine light springs from divine love which is: "let there be light." This is the beginning. The light lights everything for man in order that he might become aware of the light. Perceiving the light awakens love of the light, of the truth, a love which distinguishes itself from all darker manifestations. Love of the truth awakens love of the truth and light of other human beings. It awakens love which does not yet exist in order that it might "become." This is to do the truth.[58]

Naiveté stands in the way of love. It knows only a ready-made, finished world, which exists without the knowing subject. Thereby it excludes the primal beginning.

To feel the other's feelings in the same way as I can think his thoughts — to feel that the other feels what I feel — causes love to stream forth, not the feeling of surfaces, friction at the surfaces and separateness. Here is the source of the fundamental social law according to which everyone works for others. In fact, through the division of labor, this is already given. But to realize this consciously, with all its consequences, would be the solution to the problems of man and mankind.

Only the quest for truth, for cognition, only service to the truth and to cognition in which the ego has no part except that it must be overcome, and that its force must transform itself into what it was originally, cognitive power, can bring harmony to man. The search for truth, for cognition, educates one in the overcoming of egoism, not by fighting it, but by seeing through it. This victory opens man's creative force to the way of love. Acting out of love is the only living possibility for humanity. For this to happen, care for the truth must be nurtured so that one loves not by following his ego, but by following the truth. This is one and the same thing. Indeed, since truth is not knowable by the ego, it would be useless to try to communicate the truth to it. The truth has been spoken: "You will know the truth, and the truth will make you free." The truth will lead you to love, to *cháris*. Where *alétheia* is realized, there *cháris* can appear. The gesture of searching for the truth is already the gesture of love. The gesture of giving up "me" and "mine." "Thy will be done." Each gesture that receives, that speaks for the sake of the other, is a gesture of love.

Actions may arise from manifold sources: laws, interests, habits. *Cháris* means that they arise out of moral intuition; therefore out of freedom. Grace (*cháris*) does not mean that our actions are unnecessary.

Alétheia springs from *cháris*; and so, in order to attain *cháris*, man must first realize *alétheia*. But this does not mean that a ray of *cháris* cannot sometimes reach him in his daily consciousness.

The capacity for ordinary reflected thinking is only possible because of the *alétheia* of living thinking which, in relation to reflected consciousness, is super-conscious. This *alétheia* comes from *cháris*.

The intuition that something new is needed for the future of mankind and must happen is already the beginning of bringing this about. The greatest task is to pass this intuition on; only in this way can it be *realized*. All other attempts at its realization are vain. One must work to bring about this one and only moral intuition.

The new age consists in humanity's passing over from the stage of "taking" to the stage of "giving." It must become clear to human beings that he who gives *will* receive, and that the more he gives, the more he will receive, if he but truly *gives*. True *being* consists in such giving, which is the form of being of the hierarchies, i.e. permeation with the light of consciousness, *alétheia*, and giving, self-giving, self-sacrifice. Indeed, nothing else can be truly given except the giver himself. But to do this a person must first *be*, enter *being*, *alétheia*, truth. If a hierarchical being does not give itself *entirely*, the more it strives to receive, the more the intensity of its being is diminished; it "remains behind"; becoming, like man, ever more dependent on the world from which it wants to receive. To give oneself is the act of creation. The time when man was guided and gifted is passing; he must now nourish his existence out of himself. This is only possible by *beginning* to return the *abundance* which God gave to man as his own abundance. Therefore the new commandment is not merely one possibility among others, but the *sine qua non* of being. We live at the end of the seventh day of creation; at the end of the day of rest. The next creators will be human beings, or the world, their world, will perish. For if the creator rests, the world cannot remain in existence.

Two healings await mankind: healing from cognitive naiveté, *alétheia*, and healing from egoity, *cháris*.

The "being" of the Logos is growing and overflowing. Its overflowing is creation.

"But strive for the greater gifts of the spirit. And I will show you yet a path of abundance"[59] (1.Cor. 12.31). This is followed by the chapter on love (1.Cor. 13).

ELEVEN

John

The closure of the world, the world of the law of conservation, has been broken open by *cháris* and *alétheia*. The kingdom of the heavens has drawn near — for *cháris* and *alétheia are* the kingdom of the heavens. The gate to heaven has been opened, and it is John, the beloved disciple, who transmits this deed to us. In and by his writings St. John dwells in the human heart, awakening in us the ability to make the first beginning. John was the first man in whom religious experience and cognition, worship and awareness, were one and the same process.

The reality of the past must be made whole by *alétheia*. Not only must the past of cognition and its results be taken as reality, but cognition itself, its presence, must also be included. In this greater reality — from which it fell in the beginning — "the world of facts and objects" will be absorbed and dissolved, and one will discover that the proper reality of this world lies in the dying of the present.

The reality of the present, which is life, must be made whole by *cháris*. Cognition is not the only aspect of reality. *Cháris*, the generation of abundance out of nothing, is the strongest reality. But it is only a seed; it is the reality of the future. The world of life, of cognition, is absorbed and dissolved in this higher reality, whence it originates and is cognized. Morality, as the principle of creation, is the more primal reality; it is the act of creation which includes cognition. Morality is not added to reality, nor is it a kind of convention; it is originary—the love for what does not yet exist, that it may become! We live by the abundance of "moral intuitions." All that is around us, and we ourselves, are results of past "primal beginnings," past acts of creation performed out of love. John was always known as a messenger of love, although it is seldom understood of what kind of love he is speaking. Thus he appears in Dante's *Commedia* as the poet's "examiner" in the matter of love (*Paradiso* Canto 26).

St. John is the most personal of the Evangelists, as is his Gospel. Besides him only St. Luke, in the first four verses of his Gospel, speaks of himself, characteristically calling upon the "witnesses and ministers of the Logos from the beginning" (*ap' archés*). The other two synoptic Evangelists do not speak of themselves. But in the Fourth Gospel seven passages can be found where the author refers to himself; two of these are in the Prologue, and the third follows them directly (John 1.15). All these passages speak in the first person plural: "And the Word dwelt among us"; "And we beheld his glory" (John 1.14); "And of his fullness have we all received *cháris* for *cháris*" (John 1.16). The Prologue begins on the highest plane of existence and ends with the word "us." By this means St. John unites himself and the reader contemplating the text with the plane of existence of the primal beginning or *arché*. He unites the reader with himself and with the community of the Word, in whose name St. John says "we" and "us."

We are given a direct indication of the author in his description of the crucifixion. After the piercing by the spear, when blood and water flow out of the body of the Logos-bearer, he writes: "And he that saw it bare record, and his record is true (*alethiné*): and he knoweth that he saith true, that ye might believe" (John 19.35). Here St. John speaks about himself in the third person. The phrase "and he knoweth . . . ," difficult to understand in its ordinary meaning, points to the certainty and the *kind* of experience of a higher cognitive plane of experience which makes John the sole reporter of this scene. It is an event which was relevant only to him and which he alone was able to cognize. He refers to this in his Epistle (1.John 5.6-9), in the passage where the witnesses in heaven and on earth are listed. For this reason he emphasizes his testimony during the crucifixion.

The fifth passage is likewise impersonal in relation to the author, but personal in relation to the reader: "But these are written, that ye might believe that Jesus is the Christ, the Son of God; and that believing ye might have life through his name" (John 20.31). This sentence is repeated, almost literally, in his Epistle (1.John 5.13).

The last two references appear at the end of the Gospel, where the author makes himself known, identifying himself as the "beloved disciple": "This is the disciple which testifies of these things, and wrote these things: and we know that his testimony is true (*alethés*). And there are also many things which Jesus did, the which, if they should be written every one, I suppose that even the world itself could not contain the books that should be written" (John 21.24,25). There is a widespread theory that these two verses are not by the author but by friends or disciples who "edited" his work. This view is based mainly on the plural: "We know that his testimony is true."

The previous quotation (John 19.35) already shows, however, that the author says his testimony (*martyría*) is *alethiné*. The plural should not mislead us to a premature judgment. We have already seen the meaning; in his first Epistle, St. John mostly uses "we" instead of "I" — which we shall go into later.

Chapter 21, verse 25, renders yet further proof of St. John's authorship of the Gospel's last two verses. Here the author speaks in the first person singular, saying "I suppose." This is the only place in the Gospel where he does so. The content of this verse emphasizes that of John 20.30 and is of great consequence. Having made himself known in the preceding verse, St. John now speaks, in the last verse, in the first person singular. It is significant that this is *not* a statement requiring higher cognition. The plural "we know," on the other hand, refers to cognition on a higher plane — where the earthly individuality is irrelevant — as, for example, when it says that the testimony is based on *alétheia*, or is *alethés*, indicating a definite cognitive plane.

The statement that "we know that his testimony is true," that it comes from *alétheia*, from living, present experience, is repeated in St. John's Third Epistle (3.John 12). His First Epistle shows in a very characteristic way his consistent and meaningful use of singular and plural. The first, third, fourth and fifth part are, with the sole exception of verse 5.13 and a predicate in verse 5.16, kept in the first person plural ("we," "us") throughout. The striking "we know" of St. John 21.24 appears in the Epistle four times. (1.John 3.2; 3.14; 5.19; 5.20). The Epistle's beginning, referring almost literally to the beginning of the Gospel, testifies that its author is a "minister of the Logos." Everything is stated in the first person plural. The intention of the Epistle is also defined: "That which we have seen and

JOHN

heard declare we unto you, that ye also may have fellowship with us: and truly our fellowship is with the Father, and with his Son Jesus Christ" (1.John 1.3). In all his writings St. John aspires to this fellowship or community (*koinonía*). In the second part of the Epistle, besides "we" and "our," the first person singular appears repeatedly (1.John 2.1, 12-14,21,26): for instance, in John 5.13 — "I write unto you," "I have written unto you." It is evident from 1.John 2.11-14, that the terms "I write" and "I have written" are meant neither trivially nor without regard for meaning. The verb "write" always appears in this Epistle for a definite reason (1.John 1.4; 2.7; 5.13; etc.). It means more than simple communication. It is a kind of communion, as it were, evoking the original, sacred meaning of Scripture. For example: "But these are written, that ye might believe that Jesus is the Christ, the Son of God; and that believing ye might have life through his name" (John 20.31), and "These things have I written unto you that believe on the name of the Son of God; that ye may know that ye have eternal life, and that ye may believe on the name of the Son of God" (1.John 5.13). The writer's aim is not that one should be informed, but that one should believe and have eternal life. Understood trivially, these formulations are incomprehensible. "I write ... I have written ... because ... that ... in order to ..." these are really indications for the *reader*. They teach us *how* to read. Belief cannot be born, eternal life cannot be attained from ordinary everyday reading. Immersed in *alétheia*, the reader must "read" on the plane corresponding to the plane of the Scripture. That is to say, the text must be received as "a word of *cháris*." Then forces and capacities arise and *alétheia* and *cháris* are kindled.

From the third part of the Epistle onwards, everything is

written in the first person plural again. The reader is received by the community, the fellowship of *cháris* and *alétheia*, which is a reality not of a subjective-individual order, but a reality for all humanity. This fellowship allows the individual human being to dip into the reality of the true Church, which becomes realized in this way. In his Letters, for example in his Epistle to the Hebrews, St. Paul uses the first person plural in a similar way.

The entire *Apocalypse* is, without exception, written as John's witness or *martyría*: "I saw, I heard, I turned." The witness is named five times (Rev. 1.2,4,9; 21.2; 22.8); and the personal experience and authorship of what is revealed is emphasized throughout the entire work. The author, "I, John," who calls himself a servant of the Logos-being (Rev. 1.1) "was in the Spirit on the Lord's day" on the island of Patmos, and heard and saw and was called upon to write in a book what he had seen (Rev. 1.9). The formulation "I, John" appears again, at the end of the spiritual vision, when this reaches its climax in the appearance of the holy city of Jerusalem which descends from heaven to the earth (Rev. 21.2). In this climax it is repeatedly proclaimed that these words are certain and true and that they are meant for the servants of the Logos-being: "And I John saw these things, and heard them" (Rev. 22.8). This emphasis and the reference to his own experience show John in his role as witness, a role which belongs to him more than to any other author of the New Testament: ". . . and he sent and signified it by his angel unto his servant John" (Rev. 1.2); ". . . which we have heard, which we have seen with our eyes . . ." (1.John 1.1); "And he that saw it bare record . . ." (John 19.35); "This is the disciple which testifies of these things . . ." (John 21.24).

JOHN

The Apocalypse is St. John's most personal work: he bears full responsibility for it. No other witness exists for what is described. His vision of the future refers to the soul-spiritual possibilities of future human beings, which will of course influence humanity's outer history. His account leads us out of darknesses, through battle, dramatic super-earthly and earthly events, to the New Jerusalem, the city of light. There earthly and heavenly history (described more from the point of view of the latter) flow together. Compared to the other writings of the New Testament, this is new: a man, "I, John," sees the super-earthly meaning of the last earthly events at the end of time—a meaning striving for a new heaven and a new earth, for the city not illumined by an outer sun (Rev. 22.5).

In his letters, especially in the very elaborate *First Epistle*, John is working for the "earthly realization" of the cosmic-heavenly events described in the Apocalypse. The structure of this Epistle duplicates that of the Fourth Gospel in its emphasis on and elaboration of the theme of love, particularly the love of human beings for one another, expressed in the *cháris* passages of the Gospel and in the new commandment (John 1.14-17; 13.34; 15.12). The "beloved disciple" is authentic in this domain (John 13.23; 19.26; 21., 20,24).

The letter begins like the Gospel with the primal beginning, the Logos, the life that "appears," "that we have seen with our eyes and touched with our hands." Now, instead of the Baptist bearing witness (1.John 1.6-8), "*we* bear witness" (1.John 1.1-2). The themes of light and darkness (1.John 1.5-6) and the "doing of the truth" (1.John 1.6) follow. The essence of community is characterized: "But if we walk in the light, as he is in the light, we have fellow-

BECOMING AWARE OF THE LOGOS

ship one with another..." (1.John 1.7). The conditions are described under which truth, *alétheia*, and the Logos do not live within us (1.John 1.8-10). We recognize these themes; we found them already in the Gospel.

In the second part of the Epistle we are told that the criterion for true cognition is to act upon it (1.John 2.3-4). One who keeps the words — *lógoi* — of the Lord, in him they blossom as love. "Hereby we know that we are in him" (1.John 2.5,6). The old commandment was also his word, his Logos, "from the beginning" (1.John 2.7). The new commandment, which is true, *alethés*, "in him and in you," declares that the darkness is passing and that the true light (*alethinón*, compare with John 1.8) already shines (1.John 2.8). "The I am is the light of the world," as it says in the Gospel (John 8.12; 9.5; 12.46). Light and lovelessness are incompatible (1.John 2.9-11). To remain — *ménein*, dwelling — in the light of the Logos is truth and eternal life (1.John 2.24-25).

The third part begins with the remark that the present stage of being a child of God will one day be surpassed (1.John 3.1-2; see also John 1.13-14). Being a child of God consists in "righteousness," in the doing of righteousness (1.John 3.7-10), but it does not yet mean doing the truth. Whoever is born of God does not commit sin. One who does not love his brothers cannot be born of God; his deeds are not rooted in God. For, since the beginning, the Logos is called love for one another (1.John 3.11). In the primal beginning the Word was, "Let there be light." This Word occurred out of love, out of first beginning. Therefore light and love are one and the same reality for John (1.John 2.9-11) and therefore the love of men is equivalent to life (1.John 3.14).

The theme of love culminates in the fourth part of the Epistle: "Beloved, let us love one another: for love is God; and every one that loveth is born of God, and knoweth God. He that loveth not knoweth not God; for God is love" (1.John 4.7-8). For humanity the archetypal image of love is the Lord who gave his life for human beings (1.John 3.16); it is God who gave humanity his Son, the Logos, who had to die in this world. Through this deed alone God becomes visible, and becomes more so inasmuch as we unfold love for one another: "No man hath seen God at any time. If we love one another, God dwelleth in us, and his love is perfected in us" (1.John 4.12). This is another formulation of verse 1.18 the St. John's Gospel. Perfect love (1.John 4.17-18) gives birth to the reality of the world, the new earth and the new heaven, and casts out fear, which is the deficiency and corruption of human nature in contrast to the abundance of *cháris*.

The Epistle's fifth part gives an image of the spirit: "He that believeth on the Son of God hath the witness in himself: he that believeth not God hath made him a liar; because he believeth not the record that God gave of his Son" (1.John 5.10). The spirit is one's inner witness, *martyría*. One who sees the Logos is spirit; for only spirit can behold spirit. A meditation deepening these words is given in the verse: "These things have I written unto you that believe on the name of the Son of God; that ye may know that ye have eternal life, and that ye may believe on the name of the Son of God" (1.John 5.13). Thereby to be "a child of God" is secured and confirmed as the point of departure for true prayer, "in my name." Of this prayer it is said that will be fulfilled: "Amen I say unto you, that if two of you shall be in harmony in all their doing, if they shall ask for something, it shall be done for them of my Father which is of heaven" (Matt. 18-19). "And I say unto you, Ask, and it shall be given you; seek, and ye shall find; knock, and it shall be opened unto you. For every one that seeketh findeth, and to him that knocketh it shall be opened. If a son shall ask bread of any of you that is a father, will he give him a stone? ... If ye then, being evil, know how to give good gifts unto your children: how much more shall your heavenly Father give the Holy Spirit to them that ask him? (Luke 11.9-13). "And what you will ask in my Name, that I will do..." (John 14.12 and John 15.7; 16.23-26; 1.John 3.22-24; 1.John 5.14-15; James 1.5-6 and 17).

What does one ask for? One asks for the Holy Spirit, for nothing else is needed. This will certainly be given to one if one can ask for it. Indeed, to ask is itself already to be inspired by the spirit. And one to whom this spirit is given lives in the present—"of the *pneûma* of *alétheia*." For him the fabric of the world is dissolved; he makes it anew, according to the spirit, following the intuition of love, of *cháris*.

The point of departure, *alétheia*, the abiding or dwelling in the truth, in life, must be maintained. This means guarding oneself against all idolaltry (1.John 5.21), and especially from all that is not "speaking." Since man is now endowed with the Logos, it is only through the Logos that he can find what is worthy of worship.

Perfect love is mentioned four times in the Epistle: "But whoso keepeth his word, in him verily is the love of God perfected" (1.John 2.5); "If we love one another, God dwelleth in us, and his love is perfected in us" (1.John 4.12); "Herein is our love made perfect, that we may have boldness in the day of judgment..." (1.John 4.17); "There is no fear in love; but perfect love casteth out fear: because fear hath torment. He that feareth is not made perfect in love" (1.John 4.18).

The word *téleios*, perfect — from *téleio*, to fulfill — is part of the essential quality of the *cháris*. At the end of the Sermon on the Mount, after the deeds of abundance and unconditional giving have been described, the commandment is given: "Be ye therefore perfect, even as your Father which is in heaven is perfect" (Matt. 5.48). To the wealthy young man it is said: "Yet lackest thou one thing . . ." (Luke 18.22). In St. Matthew's Gospel the expression is: "If thou wilt be perfect . . ." (Matt. 19.21). The *lack*, the deficiency, is compensated by *giving*: the young man was supposed to give his great fortune away. Paul says of love: "But when that which is perfect is come, then that which is in part shall be done away" (1.Cor. 13.10). "And above all these things put on love, which is the bond of perfectness" (Col. 3.14). It is perfect, complete reality. This requires *cháris*, continuous creation out of nothing or, in other words, love that is creative and that alone is love. The image of creative building-up is the plant, which gives much fruit: "I am the vine ye are the branches. He that abideth in me and I in him, the same bringeth forth much fruit: for without me ye can do nothing" (John 15.5).

In the Epistle we find the only place in the New Testament where the verb "to love" is used without an object as a categorical reality (1.John 3.18; 4.7,8). It is characteristic of St. John's Gospel, in contrast to the other Gospels, that it does not contain any parables. There seem to be two exceptions, the good shepherd (John 10.1-30) and the true vine (John 15.1-8), but these turn out to be descriptions of the Logos-being, the I am: "I am the good shepherd. . . . I am the true vine. . . ." Instead of parables in words we find parables in deeds: the washing of the feet (John 13. 1-20), the writing on the ground (John 8.8), the transformation at the marriage at Cana (John 2.1-11), and perhaps also the healing of the man blind from birth (John 9). Most importantly, these parables are spoken in the language of cognition, of higher knowledge. Such is the nature of the Prologue, of the conversations with Nicodemus and the Samaritan Woman, the addresses to the Jews in Chapters 5,6,7,8.10 and 12, and to the disciples in Chapters 13,14,15 and 16, as well as the prayer to the Father in the seventeenth chapter.

John gives the clearest statements on the Logos, the Son, the Father and the Spirit, and also on all that concerns humanity as well. In many ways the text appears as a further development of the doctrine of the Logos which had existed in various traditions since Heraclitus. This does not mean, however, that John drew on a tradition. He did not need to, since direct contact with the Logos-being, his intuitive ability, revealed all the elements of the teaching to him.

The unique spiritual configuration of St. John emerges clearly from both the Gospel and the Epistle. In him, religious experience, the adoration of the source of existence and knowledge, is one with the cognition of the eternal "object" of religious experience.[60] This unity of religious experience and cognition lived only briefly in the following centuries, and religious and cognitive life have continued along separate paths until today. The uniqueness of St. John's experience results from his close connection to the earth. In spite of the highest spiritual experience, he is concerned with the earth, the future of the earth and the earthly destiny of mankind: this is the purpose of his Apocalypse and his teaching of *alétheia* and *cháris*, his path through *alétheia* to love. Thereby he becomes the Apostle of the new love, the new heaven and the new earth, formed from the blossoming of the human ability to love, *cháris*.

Where he describes this reality, we find the phrase of the Logos-being, "It is done"—literally, "it has become," *gégonen*. (Rev. 21.6). Something that never "was" from eternity, has become an earthly-cosmic reality. A *new* heaven, *new* earth, "for the first heaven and the first earth have passed away" (Rev. 21.1). We saw in Chapter 4 how much John insists that Jesus is the Christ (1.John 2.22; 4.2-3,15; 5.5), that the Logos of the cosmos dwelt in a human body and passed through death and was resurrected in this body. When Lazarus already lay in the earth, in the mineral element, and was called forth from thence through the word of the Logos-being, a deep transformation took place in this element that had been foreign to the Godhead until then. The Logos-being took it into his essence: "and the Logos became flesh." This is, on the one hand, the beginning, *arché*, of the redemption of the mineral and, on the other hand, the redemption of the intellect. The intellect depends entirely on the mineral in man. Reflected consciousness means that physical-mineral processes in the brain accompany the process of consciousness. Intellect is the consciousness of what is past, of consciousness's past, or dead content. The living subject looks at these from its eternal present, but forgets itself—*léthe*. The continuity of consciousness is constantly interrupted, a continuous dying takes place in consciousness, and the transition from what is living to what is dead is not experienced—*that* is death. The mineral is the final stage, the coming to rest of the process which is not experienced. For pre-Christian consciousness minerality is impenetrable. Spiritual schools striving for higher knowledge bypass it; for them cognition occurs outside the mineral-physical

159

body. After the intermediate stage of the Baptist with his baptism in water comes baptism with fire and the spirit. This links the process of higher cognition with the penetration and metamorphosis of the physical body, making higher cognition possible. Herein lies the battle for man's existence: Is the higher principle capable of penetrating the body "from above" in such a way that the body—and thereby the earth —becomes the image and expression of the spirit? Or do the spirit and the body remain in the end foreign to one another? The adversaries of man would like to prevent this permeation. The lord of the world of the past would like to solidify this "past-world" entirely. The spirit of egoity, who "remained behind" because of his incomplete self-sacrifice, would like to tear the human soul away from what is earthly, but in such a way that the soul would maintain its selfhood, and thereby join and increase the particular soul-spiritual world which reflects the characteristic property of this Spirit.

The appearance of the Greek gods in human form is basically a tentative attempt to answer the question of whether the divine, the higher principle, can really become human. This question, which concerns the destiny of the cosmos, is answered by "... and the Logos became flesh," and by the event following the burial, the permeation of the earth by the Logos, through whom all was created except for what is dead in the mineral: *visitabis interiora Terrae*, "you will visit the interior of the earth" (Tabula Smaragdina).[61] *This* event brings about the light on earth whereby the earth begins to become a sun. This light is the light of human cognition by which humanity, through natural science, to begin with, is about to penetrate the mineral element. For man to become a sun-being, to kindle his inner sun, this light shall and must grow: in this way the earth becomes the sun.

160

JOHN

The mineral is necessary to develop the human intellect. The intellect is necessary for man to achieve self-consciousness. Self-consciousness is necessary to distinguish oneself from what is dead. The distinction between oneself and what is dead is the first step toward the re-enlivening of self-consciousness. The entrance of consciousness into life is the prelude for the unfolding of *cháris*, human love on earth, which is the earth's goal, and for which all obstacles are necessary.

In the New Testament St. John teaches the transubstantiation in the greatest detail. His Gospel is the only one in which a transformation of matter is described: the marriage at Cana. The secret of the Last Supper is not described in the scene of the Last Supper (John 13), but is described at length in the sixth chapter (John 6.35-38), while the central themes in the thirteenth chapter are the washing of the feet and the new commandment.

John is a builder of the future — a future not only in the temporal sense — both in his Apocalypse and in his Gospel and in his Epistles. The expression "doing the truth" (John 23.21; 1.John 1.6) refers to "a world to come," not to an existing world; the same applies to: "setting one's seal that God is true" (John 3.33) or "making God a liar" (1.John 1.10; 5.10).

In earlier times it was the task of the gods or of the messengers of the gods to prepare the future of man and mankind. In John we see man taking over this task from the hands of the gods, from the hands of the Son of God: "If I will that he — John — tarry till I come, what is that to thee?" (John 21.22). The significance of this lies in that man has now come of age and must determine his future by himself. John brings this originally divine mission down to man. This is why he emphasizes so insistently that his testimony is true—because it comes from higher cognition. The Apocalypse is like the opening of a gate, the gate of the future: "After this I looked, and, behold, a door was opened in heaven..." (Rev 4.1).

The two Johns, the Baptist and the Evangelist, often depicted together, have a mysterious connection with one another. The Baptist announces the approaching of the kingdom of heaven: "Change your mind (Repent): for the kingdom of heaven is at hand" (Matt. 3.2). But the Baptist himself does not enter the kingdom of heaven: "... he that is least in the kingdom of heaven is greater than he" (Matt. 11.11); he is not the light (John 1.8). The approach of the kingdoms of heaven means that the worlds of cognition, of the spirit, which were formerly accessible only in ecstasy, by lifting the human soul out of increasing I-naturedness, have grown closer to the I. Men will be able to experience these worlds of cognition in that they rise from and outgrow their everyday I.[62] *Metanoeîte*—change your spiritual temper, your spiritual attitude, and you will be able to experience the kingdoms of heaven in a different way. When the Baptist is captured and beheaded, the working of the Logos-being changes (Matt. 4.12-17 and 14.1-13).

In St. Mark's Gospel the account of the Apostles' mission is dramatically interrupted by the account of the destiny of the Baptist (Mark 6.7-29). The text then continues: "And the apostles gathered themselves together unto Jesus, and told him all things, both what they had done, and what they taught" (Mark 6.30). This indicates that forces, which were working in the Baptist, passed over into the disciples. Amongst the disciples John the Evangelist seems to stand in a particular connection to the Baptist. As the Baptist belongs to the descending line of the Sign of Cancer, "I must decrease, he must increase" (John 3.30), the Evangelist represents the rising line. The Baptist represents the past, the Evangelist the future. The Baptist "becomes" predestinately (John 1.6; Mark 1.4), the Evangelist forms himself through inner development in the human life of his time. They share characteristic themes. Firstly, they have in common the theme of the bridegroom (John 3.29; Rev. 18.23) and the bride (Rev. 21.2; 22.17). For the Baptist, the bridegroom is a symbol; he stands beside it as an onlooking friend; but for the author of the Apocalypse the bridegroom is the being of the world who unites with mankind, the bride. These themes appear (except for the wedding at Cana) only at the above-mentioned places. The second theme that they share is the "Lamb of God" (John 1.29, 36 and in the Apocalypse at various places as the main theme). The Baptist sees the Lamb that redeems the consequences of human sin. The Apostle of the Apocalypse sees the Logos-being as the prototype and proto-warrior for wisdom and the overcoming of evil. In the New Testament this theme of the Lamb appears only in St. John's Gospel.

The numerous differences between the two John figures have a polar quality. The Baptist teaches an *initiatio*, a "wisdom of the beginning" — Paradise themes abound in his sayings: tree, fruit, snake. The Evangelist points to the fulfillment — *teleiosis* — of wisdom, and in the Apocalypse he heralds a *city* as the sign of redeemed humanity.

The Baptist, the hermit in the solitude of the desert, unfamiliar with the material world, wears the same clothes and eats the same food as Elijah (Matt. 3.4 and 2.Kings 1.8). The Evangelist teaches transubstantiation (Cana), speaks of the true bread, the true drink, the true vine. The Baptist dies, the beloved disciple "remains." The one dies young, the other in old age. The element of the one is water, the other in old age experiences his great revelation on the solid earth of the Isle of Patmos. The one dies because of a woman, Herodias, who stands diametrically opposed to the highest, pure feminine principle, *Sophia,* the "Mother of Jesus." In comparison with the Logos, Sophia is the older spiritual principle that appeared in human consciousness and prepared for the idea of the Logos.[63] She is the element of the wisdom of the heart, whence the lighter, more conscious element of the Logos springs. In the modern sense, she is the purified, prepared human soul, who can go to meet and receive the spirit of the worlds.[64] Below the Cross the beloved disciple is united with this element by the dying Logos-being: "Then saith he to the beloved disciple, Behold thy mother! And from that hour that disciple took her into his self-being" (John 19.27). Thus, the two *witnesses* stand side by side, related and polarized.

St. John's Tide falls in the middle of the year, close to the longest day. The grouping of the blessed in Dante's *Paradiso,* in the white rose, gives the Baptist what he could not attain, his connection with the mother of Jesus. The Mother of God takes her seat in the highest rank in the rose, but the Baptist has his seat opposite to her in the circle, equally in the highest rank, the furthest away from her, but facing her in eternal contemplation. In the same way St. John's Tide and Christmas, the festival of the birth-giving human soul, stand opposite each other in the cycle of the year.

TWELVE

The Teaching of the Logos and Spiritual Science

"In the beginning was the Logos." Once habits of everyday consciousness are overcome, this sentence seems a simple, self-evident truth, the beginning of all truths. For in the first inner stirring of an I-consciousness, the Logos is already present as the first and only born, and present with it are the two other realities of creative consciousness, *cháris*, the ability for active, productive love, and *alétheia*, the ability to cognize what is concealed. It only takes *one* person to understand and describe all this for the kingdom of heaven to draw near for all humanity, for human beings gradually to begin to rise from their everyday consciousness to *alétheia* and *cháris*. For as soon as these realities are formulated and expressed as ideals, reflected consciousness has a point of departure for the path to these realities themselves.

The two higher spheres of reality lying closest to everyday consciousness are called *cháris* and *alétheia*. These were not unknown in earlier, pre-Christian times and had names then also. John, however, for the first time gives them human designations, which are to a certain degree accessible to everyday consciousness, and therefore attainable. For if one wishes to live as a *human* being, one needs truth and unconcealment. These are not given to one by nature, one must take pains to achieve them. Precisely this effort is human and makes a person human. *Cháris*, "grace," likewise means "not by nature"; and this points to its source, which lies above everyday consciousness and "comes from above." Both ideas are connected with man — only for human beings can "truth" and "grace" exist.

Alétheia and *cháris* are names for experiences, names given by the one who cognizes them. As realities of mind and heart they are called life (*zoé*) and love (*agápe*). These are the kingdoms of the heavens, which have drawn near to man, even in their designations. They have drawn near through the Logos consciousness of the experience through the spirit. John becomes the inaugurator of the new epoch of consciousness, and he is conscious of it. If "read" on the corresponding plane of consciousness, his writings educate man for the experience described in them. During the event of Pentecost the Spirit flows over upon Christ's prepared disciples.

The approach of the kingdom of heaven means that man is virtually able to cognize everything. Thereby his Logos increases — and, at the same time, he can overcome egoity with new earthly human love. This love is a human creation. It makes possible the *beginning* of a new building of the world, which otherwise passes away. This passing away means not only the exhaustion of the gifts and treasures of the earth, but also the drying up of the natural connection of man with his intuitive source, the creative world, the world of the gods. From now on "... no man cometh unto the Father but by me" (John 14.6). Since his first permeation by the breath of the Divine (Genesis 2.7), man can

THE TEACHING OF THE LOGOS AND SPIRITUAL SCIENCE

now, in Christianity, be imbued, for a second time, with the Word. This Word:

> is, or at least should be, a reduplication of its content, which is at the same time the condition for its being reflected. It is reduplicated again, insofar as man not only has the Word, but also has a relation to the Word, and a relation to the fact that he has the Word. This means that he not only *has* the Word which determines his consciousness, but that this consciousness reduplicates in relation to the Word. It also means that he can become aware of the fact that he partakes of the Word. Thereby, out of his being's bondedness *to* the Word, he enters freedom *in* the Word. Here the deep connection between the Word and self-consciousness becomes apparent. If man can never find a relation to the Word, then *his* word, which remains nevertheless a reduplication of its content, becomes the revelation of being unbeknownst to him. For all his having lost "spirit and speech," an himself remains connected to the Word.[65]

Primal speech, which always improvises, consists only of sounds and corresponds both to the inhalation of the divine breath and to unreflected, living consciousness. Disintegrating into many word-languages, in which each word has a determined meaning, the Tower of Babel is built. Improvisation comes to an end. But, nevertheless, archetypal speech still resounds through word-languages, "somehow" making possible understanding between people of different languages without translation or an interpreter.

Christianity had a twofold result. Firstly, man became free in relation to the Word; and secondly, precisely through this liberation, he gradually became able to adapt the word-language to the expression of a living — improvised — thinking and perceiving. Although words are often "crust-like" they can be used so as to always yield a new meaning according to the context in which they are used. If used in this way language becomes appropriate once more for the expression of living reality and the reality of love.

Men can reach the kingdoms of heaven, which are "at hand," in two stages. Overcoming "*this world*" means experiencing it in its living reality, in becoming and "unbecoming," in *alétheia*. "*Doing the truth*" — making the truth — means creation out of nothing: deeds of love. This creation also gives birth to the cognition of present reality. Such "doing" is the reality of the future, without which the world is incomplete — not *téleios*. Both steps depend on "realizing the Son" as described in Chapter Six. If the Son is not cognized, or disappears from human consciousness, the two seeds of reality inaugurated by St. John will be lost, and not fulfilled.

The reader of the Gospels and of the Fourth Gospel in particular is given a clear picture of the difficulties in grasping the idea and reality of the Son of God, who is at the same time the Son of Man, the flower of humanity, whose essence he brought forth. It is therefore understandable that within a few centuries the idea of the Son was lost in the Christian Church. Indeed, since that time there is little reason for the Church to be called "Christian." The clear distinction between Jesus and Christ, together with the simultaneous consciousness of their temporary identity, so strongly emphasized by St. John, had already disappeared by the fourth century. The Cosmic Christ, Logos, or Countenance of God, the Word-reality of every I-being and the Logos-reality of the world, were no longer understood. To earlier, younger humanity, the world "spoke." Objects gave their idea as they were being perceived, they "said" what they were, and thereby they "became" a specific thing. Such speaking was the divinity of the world. It was an illumined world and one could therefore seek and find the Godhead in the things of the world. Then, in the Dark Age, the *Kali Yuga*, the speaking died away and the original light of the world faded. After that, it was the silence itself that directed men like Abraham to the coherent unity of the world's ground. Soon, however, the experience of this union lost its liveliness, became abstract, and could no longer be expressed. It became *unspeakable* and therefore, except for a few chosen individuals, people in general could no longer address this world ground. Thus it continued until the turning point of time when the intuition of the Word, the Logos, appeared to a few human beings although it was potentially valid for all, especially the poor, the sick and the "sinners." This means that things are not "merely" things — but are words, ideas, and are only thereby truly "things." It means that man can now see the Word, the "Word-Light," even in this world; because "the Logos became flesh."

To have lost the idea of the Son means a reversion — into Judaism at best — and is therefore untimely, because Christianity has had its effect upon man, and the new capacities exist without being appropriately used by him. Therefore they are used by forces inimical to him, against him, against the goal of humanity and the earth. Corresponding to the two possibilities of *alétheia* and *cháris*, two diseases of consciousness spring up: agnosticism instead of gnosis (cognition) and determinism instead of love.

Agnosticism has many faces, all of them based on the conviction that the world is not "word-natured," but wordless, without ideas, "non-speaking" — that concepts and words are entities, added by man to reality which exists without him. Cognition has no reality; it is only nominal. Therefore one speaks about what is unknowable in general or about certain realities which cannot be known. These are all variations on the theme: there is no cognition; cognizing is not a real process. It makes no great difference whether the unknowable is imagined as a divine world or as a material reality inaccessible to cognition. Thus the medieval doctrine that it is impossible to know the truth of revelation is a predecessor of today's cognitional naiveté. For how does one know about revelation, if one cannot cognize it? *To whom* is revelation given? And *for whom* does the material world, about which humanity has so much to say, exist? Although materialism often appears not to be agnostic, cognition is only of "nominal" value for materialism, because ideas and concepts have no ontological existence. Nominalism, the view that the word and the idea have nothing to do with the essence of a thing, is the natural consequence of the fact that, after a brief period of light, mankind once more lost the idea of the Logos, the being that reveals, or in today's language, the idea of cognition. The Son loses his essential particularity, and his essential being can no longer be distinguished from that of the Father. The cosmic Logos becomes the simple Nazarene. And, since the Son is lost, it is not astonishing that the independent spirit in man—his ability to perceive the Logos—is also dogmatically removed in 869. With this event, the way to the de-humanization of man is open. Even before Mohammed, Christianity had become "Islamic" to a great extent: it no longer knew the Son. "Allah has no Son"—this is one of the most important, central dogmas of the Koran.[66] Allah is an unapproachable, uncognizable, unfriendly God, to whom humanity means nothing; his world is complete without human beings. When Allah so desires he leads man into error; man is powerless to resist this guidance, and then is punished for his error. According to the Koran, cognition means as little as it does to the empiricist Francis Bacon. Man should limit himself to the observation of things and phenomena, as if an entire world of ideas, which selects *what* is to be observed, did not have to precede every observation. Natural science arose only after Newton had created the necessary scaffolding of ideas out of pure thinking; only then could one know what to observe.[67]

This modern disease of consciousness was prefigured very graphically in a tale by Rumi, the Islamic mystic of the thirteenth century:

> A seeker knocked at the door of the beloved — God — and a voice from inside asked: "Who is it?" The seeker answered: "It is I"; and the voice said: "In this house there is no I and You." The door remained locked. Then the seeker went into solitude, fasted and prayed. A year later he returned and knocked at the door. Again the voice asked: "Who is it?" Now the believer answered: "It is You." Then the door opened.

One could appreciate the mystical self-denial of this story for its truth and beauty, if the believer would had only included himself as the *speaking* personality when he said, "It is You." But the general tenor of Islam as well as the Arabic influence on European spiritual life militate against this. The dispute between the Averroists and the Scholastics reflects this conflict, and modern spiritual life suffers from it too. The thinker considers only the finished thought, the logic of thought, and does not reckon with the reality of thinking and the thinker himself. Therefore a sentence like

"I am not" or "You are not" can today be experienced as logical. This was introduced in Europe for the first time by Arabistic thinkers. The Averroists claimed that the individual intellect has no ability to cognize the supersensible; that the essence of consciousness is different from that of the spiritual world; that the spirit is different in essence from the consciousness which thinks and conceives it; that the everyday I has no relation to the eternal I; that the I dissolves after death into the Godhead. But it is the everyday I that asserts all this. The question is: if the content of such statements is true, how can one know it, how can it be cognized? This would have been the reply of the Scholastics. But Thomas Aquinas himself, infected by the doctrine of "twofold truth," was unable to ask this question. And today's scientists do not ask it either. "Man is nothing but . . . , thinking is nothing but . . . , the spirit is nothing but . . ."— and then follows everything that is not man, thinking or spirit, without the realization that, it is always either man, thinking or the spirit which is *speaking*. Therefore they testify *against themselves*. This is the counter-image of the Logos-being who bears witness of himself as the light of the world. The spirit sins against itself; this is the sin against the Holy Spirit, which cannot be forgiven from without. Only the spirit itself, already immanent, can redeem *this* sin.

Nominalism assumes that thinking is identical with words, that there is no thinking without words. Nominalism forgets that words receive their meaning from and through thinking, and does not see that this *something*, to which a word refers, must already be *that*. To get a name, a thing must first be an "idea." The belief that anything could exist without an idea is anti-Logos. This tendency also prevails in Islam.

Naiveté is the common trait of all diseases of consciousness out of which have arisen both the dogma that there can be a reality without cognition and the doctrine of a spirit which one cannot know.

Instead of *alétheia*, we still have naiveté, which is a pre-Christian attitude of consciousness. According to this, cognition does not add anything to reality. This was fine as long as cognition was not human cognition, and therefore not true *cognizing* at all, since the concept of cognizing as such did not yet exist and what we would call cognition still meant a participation in the world of light. What early humanity received through perception, and through a kind of inspiration which worked in the place of thinking, the human being today must—or should—strive for independently. Were he to do so, he would be capable of acquiring everything through contemplation in a self-conscious way.

Early man, for whom self-contemplation was still impossible as well as unnecessary, received not only his ideas and thoughts through perception and inspiration, but also the impulses for his acts. To him the world and things in the world were not merely what they are for modern man, they still contained concepts. This fact is the basis of today's striving for cognition. Moreover, they still had a moral quality as well. Nowadays, one can no longer even ask what makes it possible to "know," what constitutes the act of cognition, etc., but for early man the meaning of a natural object or phenomenon was its idea or function in the universe as a whole. This also included what the creative Godhead wanted from man—what the Godhead expected from man in relation to the object.[68]

When the language of nature fell silent, the inspiration for human activity also came to an end. The impulses for action now began to flow from other sources. In addition to inspiration by the will of the gods, as mediated by the priests and rulers, egoity now began to awake — primarily of course among the mediators of the divine will, for they were closest to I-consciousness. Until the nineteenth century this egoity was something of which man was ashamed, because he experienced it as a corruption of his original nature. Man, awakening to I-consciousness, felt impelled in his deeds by extra-human sources and experienced this as pre-determined destiny, or predestination. One could ask those who think thus: Is your statement that man is predestined itself predetermined? If the statement is to have any truth at all, the answer can only be "no"; thereby the asserted statement is annulled, at least with regard to the process of cognition; and from that point on its validity is altogether dissolved. All determinists of course ought to be asked this question.

It is clear that the determinist, or the adherent to a doctrine of predestination, holds a pre-Christian attitude, but holds it with the means of modern man, with I-consciousness. However, in his very understanding (cognition) of determinism and predestination he goes beyond what can be predetermined, and thereby contradicts himself and so bears witness against himself. Modern man adds to this picture of the human being the principle of "natural" egoity, and "appeals" to the fact that man is basically egotistic, i.e. "evil" in the sense of the Church. One must also ask those who make this assertion, how does the "evil" person notice his evilness? Is he still prey to his egoism when he cognizes his egoity?

Cognitional naiveté can only imagine a world which is finished without human activity. There is no place for morality in this world, because the impulses to act are basically rooted in "inborn" egoity. Man is thereby locked into a specific stage of development: there is a definite human "nature" and man cannot essentially change it. These views, too, which are those of naiveté or agnosticism, also derive from the opinions, far removed from the Logos, of the Christian churches.

In order to reach self-consciousness man had to pass through ego-consciousness, through egoity. Since ancient times he was educated by his guides to this end. Wherever and whenever anything was taught, regardless of the content of the teaching, the guide called upon the I-being of man, appealed to the I, and thereby led human consciousness along the paths which lead to I consciousness. For where man speaks — and he must speak in words — I and You must be present; they are called into being by speech. Paradoxically, therefore, those teachings which seem to attempt to dissolve the I, appeal to this I, and call it into life. It is not the content of the teaching which is important, but the fact that it is *taught*. This has always been true, and is still so today. "You have no Buddha-nature" (i.e. no spiritual being in you) the Zen-Master answers the questioner, thereby pointing directly to, and calling into the present, the Buddha-nature of the one who asks the question. If he really had no Buddha-nature there could be neither question nor answer between master and student.

The greatest difference between pre-Christian and later times lies in the capacity for the true I. In pre-Christian times only a few chosen people could strive for this capacity; in our times it has become available for the whole of humanity — or will be available soon. Potentially, it already belongs to everyone. This is the basis of democracy. In attempts at its realization — for instance, in the French

Revolution—there lives a dimly held idea of the possibilities of a consciousness common to all men. From this arises the contemporary form of "teaching," science, which basically everyone can acquire, because it works with reflected everyday consciousness, by means of which everything else is done.

In this age of extreme cognitional naiveté and the consequent victory of the principle of egoity comes a teaching which extends the "boundaries" of cognitional ability to an unlimited degree and shows that modern man can have the intuition of the true and the good. This teaching describes itself as a science, a *science of the spirit*, and is developed by its founder out of dialectical everyday consciousness. Rudolf Steiner's *Philosophy of Freedom*,[69] his most comprehensive philosophical work, begins with the investigation of thinking as the primary human tool, by means of which the human being approaches everything else. Contemplating one's thinking, one becomes aware that it is a thinking about the past, because, in thinking, it is what has been *thought* that becomes conscious, not the process of thinking itself. But past thinking cannot become *experience*, because, by the time it enters consciousness, it is already "dead." Therefore no reality can be attributed to this "thinking," which is actually only past thought. Only something that is present and living can be experienced as reality. For dead thinking the world of percepts is in itself a finished reality—one sleeps through the process of thinking, which contributes to the formation of the picture. This is how the naive world-view comes into being.

Today's ordinary consciousness, however, can be trained to experience its own present consciously. Living thinking, the origin of dead thought, can become experience. Through purely logical thinking—the kind we use in mathematics—one can grasp this process and, through appropriate and relatively simple exercises of consciousness, *experience* it. First, corresponding concepts are developed at the dialectical stage of consciousness by means of intuitions of thought such as every "normal" person is capable of. After this, one graduates to experiments in consciousness and to experience itself. One reaches the stage of consciousness of life, or truth, *alétheia*. Here the consciously witnessed process of cognition is reality. It is life, the *present* of the world. Naiveté of consciousness is first overcome conceptually, and then in experience. Truth—unconcealment—consists in man's ability to attain living truth.

One can reach living reality first through the experience of pure thinking, that is, in the phase when it is present and alive. The living present can be experienced; but its past, what is dead, can only be remembered. With the experience of living reality one reaches the "word character" of the world; for it is a Logos-world, it *speaks*. Nothing is unknowable. One must only ask: *what* is unknowable? To answer is already the beginning of cognition.

The living truth is not "correctness," but an ever deeper "illuminating" of what is concealed. Spiritual science establishes in a scientific, exact manner the possibility of knowing worlds which are closed to man by his ordinary intellectual consciousness. The way to experience these worlds by means of exercises of consciousness is described equally exactly. Thereby spiritual science becomes a science of extended cognition.

Clearly, if he "lives" with his consciousness in the world of the past, man is not free and cannot add anything of an essential nature to the finished world. He can discover the "past" character of his mental pictures or representations and thereby can become aware that he is not a part of this world of the past. He is the one who discovers it, who lives in the present, but does not experience it. From here, the path opens to the *experience* of "present."

Instead of pursuing this possibility, however, man today is intent on including himself in this ascertained world of the past. He discovers the mineral, the animal, the not-good, and asserts, I myself am mineral and animal. He does not realize that he is none of these things, because it is his dualistic consciousness which enables him to notice them.[70] This is the same witnessing against oneself which has been described earlier.

In the finished world of naive realism—and every form of realism is "naive"—man also is "finished." He cannot develop himself out of himself any further; therefore he is not responsible for himself either, and so loses the most valuable gift he could have: the possibility of further creating himself and the world. In fact, he renounces the human privilege of never being "finished," of never finishing. For *man is not*, he can only become, and in becoming—in being present—he becomes and remains man. In the process of cognition man is given the possibility of realizing himself by the path of developing his own consciousness. The possibility of moral intuition enables man to continue the creation of the world. This ability is described in the second part of the *Philosophy of Freedom*, while the first part is dedicated to healing cognitive life.

Even in its everyday aspect, cognition is fed by the sphere of life. Through his intuitive ability man is connected with this sphere, otherwise he could neither speak nor learn, think, nor perform thinking itself.

The most important result of spiritual scientific investigation is the discovery that the sphere of moral intuition — *cháris* — also becomes accessible to modern man, as he gradually removes obstacles with which he is hiding this sphere from himself. In the same way that one can have intuitions of thought — which is confirmed by the mere *existence* of science rather than by its content — one can have intuitions of goodness. First comes the intuition that goodness as such is a reality, independent of my point of view and my personal opinion as to whether it is good *for me*. One could not say that man is evil by nature, or not good, or morally indifferent if one did not have the idea of what is good or moral.

What is called *conscience* is the ability for moral intuition; but this ability is crippled in its spontaneity, in its capacity to act in the present, by the establishment of inner norms. Figuratively speaking, the ability for moral intuition is conscience, which, in every situation, in every moment, through always new intuitions, "tells" one what to do. Basically, there is only a single moral intuition: the new commandment. It has no concrete content. Because its reality is in the second heaven, it is abstract. Everyday consciousness can only notice the shadow of its shadow. By means of moral imagination this intuition is drawn from its high abstract sphere down to "this world," to the earth. In "this world" each individual situation needs a new intuition in order to be solved.

It is the tragedy of modern man that, without giving himself an account of it, he implicitly recognizes science as the common, human cognitive sun, with the task of solving all problems scientifically. For his actions, however, this form of cognition is not enough. Science only indicates the best way to attain an already *given* aim, but it does not determine the aim. Generally man chooses his aims according to the principle of what is good for himself, i.e. his egoity. Thereby the existence of a universal moral sun is denied, and each man acts according to his own nature and ideas — as is well known to be the cause of the chaos we live in and its poor prospects for the future. Because of his naive, realistic science, man is convinced that he can neither contribute anything essential to the world, nor essentially change his alleged egotistical nature; and so, resigned and fatalistic, he awaits doom in a rich selection of various catastrophes. Once the theories of science are accepted, they become true; man realizes what science predicates about him; he becomes egoistic, ruled by economic life, an evil beast. This does not have to happen, for although these "theories" are correct as diagnoses of illness, they are not norms for a healthy human being. Man holds the key in his hand: it is the intuition of *cháris* — in our language, moral intuition. Out of this intuition human beings could agree to live in accordance with it from now on. Those who are only takers could in this way become *givers*. Through *alétheia* man could know — cognize — an infinite number of new worlds thus far concealed from him; through *cháris* he could create new worlds, especially the world of love. Man has the intrinsic possibility for the creation of this world through which the earth could finally become truly Earth. Spiritual science has created a beginning for solutions of this kind in various spheres of life — in pedagogy, the social sphere, the arts, and the sciences —

beginnings which one must first understand in depth, and then develop in the context of the present situation.

In principle, anyone can understand the essential aspect of spiritual science — which is in fact the Christianity of St. John in its contemporary form. By it each human being is connected, even in his daily consciousness, with the sources of cognitional and moral intuition. From these sources one may receive "flashes of light" (insight); and by means of a path of schooling, also given by spiritual science, one may try to "remain" or "dwell" in the light. In other words, in meditation and contemplation, one can learn to *abide* in the sources of intuition, in the *experience* itself. And in this way one can both build the paths by which intuitions can reach mankind and develop these cognitional methods further for purposes of research.

What John calls *alétheia* is, in spiritual science, pure, experienced thinking. It is also, at the stage of experiencing consciousness, called *manas* or spirit-self. *Cháris*, or moral intuition, is buddhi or life-spirit.[71]

The great leaders of humanity wanted to guide all human beings to the capacity for love. This can only succeed if man becomes an "I am" being. Therefore humanity must pass — as was foreseen by all the old teachings — through the dark age of "past consciousness," mineral consciousness, egoity and lovelessness. The impulse to strive out of the darkness was given by Christianity. On the other side of the darkness, which is "already passing" (1.John 2.8), man comes to *alétheia* and to new love. After approximately 1500 years of rule by the opposite impulse — interrupted only by a few personalities of "light," mostly "heretics" — the impulse of light and love appears from its high abstract sphere in its modern form as a "science."

BECOMING AWARE OF THE LOGOS

There have always been battles between these light-impulses and love and other orientations which laid more emphasis on the *content* of a doctrine than on the process of *teaching* as such. These other orientations have two main characteristics. On the one hand, they are conservative, pointing back toward earlier states of consciousness, which are exactly what cannot be achieved; for the more one strives for such states, the more one moves away from them, because of the *striving* itself, which was unknown and nonexistent in the original states. The other distinguishing characteristic is the preservation of secret knowledge for a chosen few, who thereby assume positions of power. This is an abuse of the aristocratic social form of ancient times. Exactly these features characterize the heathen cultures of the New Testament (Matt. 20.25; Mark 10.42; Luke 22.25). Here is where Christianity distinguishes itself from ancient principles. The First Epistle to the Corinthians puts it thus: "All secret knowledge is worthless without love in man" (1.Cor. 13.2), because, without love, one is an I-less instrument, used by other forces (1.Cor 13.1).

All pre-Christian cultures, the Hebrew culture excepted, perished in the battle between the two impulses characterized above and ultimately in the victory of the conservative tendency. Our culture is about to suffer a similar destiny. Offshoots of conservatism exist today. They would keep occult knowledge secret, they have the desire for power, and the disguised aristocratism of the "super-man," who lives in the illusion of being such, while in reality he is prey to mostly sub-human instincts. These directions claim the right to be served by the "masses," but bear no responsibility towards them. The Second World War proves how dangerous these are. Nevertheless they can interfere very little with humanity's future, because they cannot cope with worldwide materialism, which is known by the East, but of which the West is not even aware. Unconsciousness in this sphere is the most prevalent, if unnoticed, disease of the conservative spiritual orientation. The latter, although nominally spiritual, is, because unaware of the Logos, in reality extremely materialistic.

A much more serious threat to the realization of the Logos would be to misunderstand spiritual science and to place the main emphasis on its content, not on the practical application and methodical exercise of the new abilities which can be acquired through it. It is a dangerous temptation naively to accept the communication of the results of spiritual scientific research as a matter of knowledge, as a "possession," and to pervert it in so doing. Such naiveté commits the same error as naive realism: one accepts words and texts as given, without realizing that they can unfold only as much meaning as one is able to grasp, to "realize" in one's consciousness. A text is always — like the whole world — only an *interpreted* text.

But since the progressive sickening of consciousness makes even the ideas and concepts of spiritual scientific communication almost impossible to understand — because the intuitive faculty for the forming of new concepts is lacking — what Rudolf Steiner feared most may happen. The scientific aspect of spiritual science could be lost; its contents could become merely applied like articles of faith — even though, in certain respects, they seem to contradict themselves — on the basis of the authority of their mediator. For example, if the reflected consciousness thinks "archangel" with the same thinking by means of which it thinks "stone," its understanding will be "inadequate" to the archangel

BECOMING AWARE OF THE LOGOS

and perhaps also to the stone. No essential, ontological process of consciousness will have occurred. As long as the idea of the archangel is not intuitively conceived as clearly as a mathematical idea, perhaps it is healthier only to think "stone."

According to the spiritual scientific theory of knowledge, if the basic concepts of spiritual science are not formed through the intuition of ideas, it is difficult or even impossible to procede to any further spiritual experiences. The description of the path of schooling itself must inevitably be misunderstood.

The issues are not knowledge and contents, but *new* abilities, the first being the ability to form new concepts through thinking intuition. Therefore most people today need a prior schooling in consciousness to remove the obstacles in the way of this intuitive capacity. They also need to work for the ability to create new experiences and "perceptions." Without this, spiritual science remains at most a plausible theory—which one can understand if one forms the corresponding concepts, and which experience later also proves to be true. But spiritual science cannot become a *science* in this way. Nor can it be pleaded scientifically by persons who have no experience besides a conceptual structure of what they wish to plead. To be a science, spiritual science requires both a cognitive faculty and a field of experience. A mathematician who is unable to *perform* a mathematical operation cannot speak about it either.

If spiritual science does not become a science it will reach the bearers of the best forces in humanity only in exceptional cases. In this distorted form, spiritual science will hardly be recognized by them as appropriate for this time.

One who does not become aware of the Son, cannot reach

the Father — he comes to Allah. One who cannot experience cognizing itself as reality, does not come to spiritual science but to an imagined, transcendent spiritual world. He will form pictures according to the pattern of the world of everyday representations, and will block the view into the world of the spirit. In this way egoity will grow but not the Logos in man, and man will be unable to gain the fruits of love.[72]

It is doubtless impossible today for everyone to follow in the footsteps of St. John the Evangelist, to tread his path in the form appropriate to our time. But it is possible for everyone to take the view of the other John, the Baptist, and to say:

> He, who is the spirit of the Logos in me, whom I perceive, must increase. I, my ego being, must decrease. I must prepare the ways and make straight the paths for Him who comes after me, whose messenger as an ego-being I am, the messenger of the light of the world which will one day bear witness of itself within me and whose testimony I shall bear in me. To prepare the paths to the world of intuition — which is at hand — means to remove the obstacles of consciousness, myself, my ego.
> Thus I will one day have the intuition of the True Man. I will be able to meet the Christ Being in the world of life.

THE END

NOTES

CHAPTER 1

1. We find two expressions for "life" in St. John's Gospel: *zoé* is natural and at the same time spiritual and eternal life, and is to be experienced with spiritual consciousness. The other term, *psyché*, designates the "life of the soul," which is attached to the life of its own particular being. See also Chapter 6 of this book.
2. Meditation begins with the kind of thinking that flows without words. It remains in the present and experiencing. This experiencing gesture is called contemplation. See also G. Kühlewind, *Stages of Consciousness: Meditations on the Boundaries of the Soul*, "Concentration and Contemplation," Lindisfarne Press (West Stockbridge, MA, 1984); and by the same author: *Die Wahrheit tun. Erfahrungen und Konsequenzen des intuitiven Denkens*, "Meditation" and "Die zweite Stufe der Meditation" (Stuttgart, 1978).
3. Concerning "Beholding of the Countenance of God" and its covering, see Chapter 4.
4. Michelangelo's painting of Creation in the Sistine Chapel of the Vatican.
5. See Chapter 8.

CHAPTER 2

6. Concerning the "decline": see *Die Wahrheit tun*, "Das Ende des Siebenten Tages."
7. The ram with its head turned back: The ram already exists in Babylonian times as a zodiacal sign, the symbol of the

BECOMING AWARE OF THE LOGOS

resurrection of nature and creative power, an attribute of the gods and the most important sacrificial animal. "Even after Christian reinterpretation the ram retains the meaning of cosmological resurrection: certain ram-lambs in the tympanum of romanesque churches must be understood as reinterpreted zodiacal signs, wherein the turned head may signify the decisive turn of the turn of the heavens. . . ." From: *Lexikon der christlichen Ikonographie*, edited by E. Kirschbaum, S.J., and others, *Allgemeine Ikonographie*, Vol. 3, catchword "*Lamm*," Vol. 4, catchword "*Widder*" (Freiburg, 1972).
8. Fragment of Heraclitus. Diels-Krantz Nr. 125.
9. *Alétheia*. See Chapters 4 and 10.
10. The prologue is considered as far as verse 14, because up to this point the text is an uninterrupted meditation. See concerning this, Rudolf Steiner, *The Gospel of St. John* (12 lectures, given in Hamburg 1908), lecture 12, Anthroposophic Press (New York, 1962, 1977). The translation given is literal and tries to keep the manifold quality of the meaning.

In verse 9 of the King James Version the "coming one" is related to "every man that cometh into the world." This is grammatically possible, but not its real meaning. Concerning this, see Chapter 4 on the *erchoménos* — "The coming one." It is a characteristic attribute of the Logos-being approaching the earth.

In verse 11 *eis tá idía* is translated as "into the individual being" and *idíoi* as "individuals" — individual human beings. The King James Version says: "He came unto his own, and his own received him not." The Greek word — the plural of the neuter form — is used by St. John several times to mean the "own being" (ego-being) of man: for example, ". . . ye shall be scattered, every man to his own . . ." (John 16.32), cf., Chapter 7; or "And from that hour that disciple took her unto his own *being*" (John 19.27) — namely Sophia; cf., the end of Chapter 11. *Eis tá idía* is probably used in the same sense in Luke 18.28 and in Acts 21.6. *Idíos* — he who has something that is his "own" — is an individual being and has individual being.

CHAPTER 3

11. The theme of "turning": The verb "to turn," "to turn around" — *strephein*, *epistrephein* — is used several times in the New Testament not in a spatial-physical sense, but as a technical term for changing the stage of consciousness: both from the everyday consciousness to supersensible consciousness and the other way around. Examples are: Matt. 16.23; Mark 8.33; Luke 9.55; Luke 22.61; John 21.20; Rev. 1.12; 1.Sam. 10.9; Gen. 19.17 and 26. On these occasions a spatial turning has no meaning at all, or no relevant meaning — and nothing is meaningless in the texts. A turning of consciousness however is meaningful; also perhaps in Matt. 9.22. In John 20.14 and 16 the meaning is very clear: Mary Magdalene "turns around" at the grave of the Lord and *sees* a figure standing and does not recognize it. When the figure speaks to her, she thinks it is the gardener. "Jesus saith unto her, Mary. She turned herself, and saith unto him, Rabboni; which is to say, Master" (16). This twofold turning signifies two different higher stages of consciousness. At the first stage Mary sees, without recognizing who it is; upon *hearing* her name she reaches the stage where she cognizes and expresses at the same time. To hear was already supersensible knowing, to speak is cognition.
12. Light is entirely ideal. Concerning this, see *Die Wahrheit tun*, "Licht-Meditationen."
13. Physics, for example, derives light from waves and particles, which have no light-nature; they would form a "dark" world. This view forgets that the point of departure was light as phenomenon. It is the un-thought: "Light is nothing but . . . no-light."

14. "Light illuminating itself" is the I am; see note 12.
15. 1.Cor. 13.12: "For now we see through a mirror, as if we were standing before a riddle, but then face to face: Now I know in part; but then shall I know even as also I am known."

    2.Cor. 13.12: "Radiance" — *dóxa* — is usually translated as "splendor, glory"; it is also "teaching" without words: the radiating effect of a being.

CHAPTER 4

16. Rudolf Steiner, *The Gospel of St. John, In Relation to the Other Three Gospels, Particularly to the Gospel of St. Luke* (14 lectures, Kassel 1909), lectures 6 and 7, Anthroposophic Press and Rudolf Steiner Press (New York and London, 1948).
17. Ibid., lecture 4.
18. Rev. 1.11. See *Novum Testamemtum, Graece*, edited by Nestle, p. 614, notes to verse 11 (Stuttgart, 1941).
19. Concerning this see Wilhelm Kelber, *Die Logoslehre. Von Heraklit bis Origines*, Chapter 2 (Stuttgart, 1976).
20. Michelangelo painted Adam just after his creation, as man *before* the fall who is still in union with the creative light; or he anticipates the future — second and *true* — Adam.
21. Note 16, lecture 7.
22. Note 16, lecture 14.
23. Lazarus: see J. Kreyenbühl, *Das Evangelium der Wahrheit*, I, pp. 157-162; (1900); and Rudolf Steiner, note 10, lecture 4.

CHAPTER 5

24. See Kelber, note 19.
25. This theme is discussed in the lecture cycle by Rudolf Steiner called *World History in the Light of Anthroposophy* (given during the foundation of the General Anthroposophical Society, Dornach, Dec. 24, 1923 until Jan. 1, 1924), Rudolf Steiner Press (London 1977).
26. See chapter 1.
27. Past-consciousness, see under note 2: *Stages of Consciousness*.

28. "My body, my soul...", concerning this, see *Stages of Consciousness*, "The Fundamental Experience of the Spirit."
29. Martin Buber, *Die fünf Bücher der Weisung. Beilage: Zu einer Verdeutschung der Schrift* (Heidelberg, 1976).
30. F. Ebner, *Fragmente, Aufsätze, Aphorismen*, page 99 (Munich, 1963).
31. In order to give a "name" to a group of phenomena, one must already "have" the group; i.e., see it clearly contoured as an idea.
32. Individual being, see note 10.

CHAPTER 6

33. Kelber (note 19), page 49.
34. "The world of life knows neither time nor space." See Massimo Scaligero, *Segreti dello Spazio e del Tempo* (Rome, 1963).
35. Qualityless matter: substances "as such" do not exist; matter is always iron, wood, etc.
36. Interruption of consciousness: when living, wordless thinking becomes thought, consciousness is interrupted — it does not follow this process. Wordless understanding flashes like lightning in verbal expression. See Chapter 10.
37. See *Die Wahrheit tun*, "Ostern."

CHAPTER 7

38. According to the teaching of the Vedas the primal state of man is the all-knowing (*Vidya*). From this man gradually sinks into not-knowing (*Avidya*). In *Avidya* man can attain knowledge only through his own effort, while it was given to him by nature in the state of *Vidya*.
39. Rudolf Steiner, *An Outline of Occult Science*, Anthroposophic Press (New York, 1970).
40. For the characterized consciousness the connections and relationships between the things and phenomena were stronger realities than the things themselves, which appeared only along with the connections.

41. Note 39, Chapter VI, "Cosmic and Human Evolution."

CHAPTER 8
42. "The death of the Logos." The paragraph can be considered as a meditation on the Rosicrucian saying: *In Christo morimur*.

CHAPTER 9
43. Characteristically the utopias of the twentieth century are mostly negative; for example, Samjakin, *Wir*; A. Huxley, *Brave New World*; G. Orwell, *1984*.
44. Matt. 25.40-45: deeds of love and compassion are the earthly realization of the logos-impulse. Therefore it says that such deeds are always done to him, and that their omission is with regard to him likewise.
45. *Homothymadón* — in unison, Acts 2.1. This expression means that obstacles in the individual, regarding the realization of the Pentecostal event, are removed, which is a precondition for this event.
46. Cognizing independent of the body: in the moment of cognizing, the process is always independent of the body, which is a *cognized object*. In contemporary everyday consciousness the body is necessary in order to *become conscious* of cognizing.
47. Cognizing is always transformation. The I of man is identified with what is to be cognized, as it is also when it knows the thoughts of another human being: one's own thinking has to think them. Sensitivity and life participate less, more dully, in this transformation; the physical body works as a mirror, as a basis of comparison — it does *not* participate; the "comparison" is the cognizing.
48. The Eightfold Path: concerning this, see Rudolf Steiner, *Knowledge of the Higher Worlds and Its Attainment*, "Some Results of Initiation," Rudolf Steiner Press (London, 1976); and *Guidance in Esoteric Training: From the Contents of the "Esoteric School,"* "For the Days of the Week," Rudolf Steiner Press (London, 1972).

49. 1. John 4.18 has been translated "because fear hath torment"; literally it means: "fear has mutilation." The King James Version translates the last word correctly as "torment," but it is not, however, very meaningful. The Greek word has both meanings.
50. For the new human community out of the present, see Rudolf Steiner, *Awakening to Community* (10 lectures given at Stuttgart and Dornach in 1923), lecture 9 of March 3, 1923, "The awakening in soul and spirit of one's fellow man," Anthroposophic Press (New York, 1974).

CHAPTER 10
51. Wordless thinking: meditation, see note 2.
52. The translation of John 1.18 is not literal, but still renders its meaning in the best possible way.
53. Ezekiel 39.29: "Neither will I hide my face any more from them."
54. See note 39, "Cosmic and Human Evolution," near the end of the chapter.
55. See Rudolf Steiner, *The Threshold of the Spiritual World*, "Concerning the Ego-Feeling and the Human Soul's Capacity for Love; and the Relation of these to the Elemental World," near the end of the chapter, Anthroposophical Publishing Company (London, 1956).
56. F. Ebner, *Schriften*, Band 1, S6.11, Verlag Kosel (Munich, 1963).
57. His reality is not on earth yet. The heavenly city has not yet come down. See Chapter 8.
58. "Doing the truth": John 3.21 and 1. John 1.6 — really "making," "creating."
59. Abundance: the word *hyperbolé* means, amongst other things, "plenty," "abundance." In the King James Version: "and yet shew I unto you a more excellent way," the essence of the idea of love has not been understood, and therefore the Greek word has not been understood either.

CHAPTER 11

60. Thus far we attempted to show various aspects of the way in which John has cognized the essence of the Logos and of the world.
61. *Rosarium philosophorum in artis auriferrae*, Vol. II, p. 253 (1593).
62. Rudolf Steiner, *The True Nature of the Second Coming*, lecture of January 25, 1910 in Karlsruhe, Rudolf Steiner Press (London, 1971).
63. Kelber, as note 19, at various places.
64. Rudolf Steiner, see note 10, lecture 12.

CHAPTER 12

65. As note 56, Vol. 1, p. 660.
66. Difficulties with regard to conceiving the essence of the Son of God: the discussions with Nicodemus and with the Pharisees, scribes and priests show clearly the dimension of these difficulties.
67. Regarding Newton: see *Die Wahrheit tun* (note 2), "Warum Geisteswissenschaft?"
68. The sense, the function of a tree? or of copper?
69. *The Philosophy of Spiritual Activity, Fundamentals of a Modern View of the World, Results of Introspective Observations According to the Method of Natural Science*, Translation by Rita Stebbing, Rudolf Steiner Publications (New York, 1963), or same book under different title: *The Philosophy of Freedom, The Basis for a Modern World Conception*, Translation by Michael Wilson, Rudolf Steiner Press (London, 1970).
70. Dualistic consciousness: everyday consciousness stands over against its "object," knows it by facing it.
71. *Alétheia* equals Manas, Spirit-Self; *Cháris* equals Buddhi, Life-Spirit. Regarding this, see: Rudolf Steiner, *Grundbegriffe der Theosophie* (14 öffentliche Vorträge, gehalten 1904/1905 in Berlin), GA 53, Ruldolf Steiner Nachlassverwaltung

(Dornach, 1957); Rudolf Steiner, *Das Christliche Mysterium* (31 Vorträge, 1906/1907 in verschiedenen Städten gehalten), GA 97, Rudolf Steiner Nachlassverwaltung (Dornach, 1968); Rudolf Steiner, *Menschheitsentwicklung und Christus-Erkenntnis. Theosophie und Rosenkruezertum. Das Johannes-Evangelium* (14 Vorträge, gehalten 1907 in Kassel, und 8 Vorträge, gehalten 1907 in Basel), GA 100, p. 196 (Dornach, 1967). Here "wisdom" — *Atma* — is also equated with the Greek "Sophia"; there is probably a mistake in the notes, since the word Sophia does not appear in the writings of St. John, whose terminology is spoken about.

72. See regarding this note 50.

Sources of the Rilke quotations opening chapters 1-9:

Rainer Maria Rilke: *Werke*. Auswahl in 2 Bänden. Insel Verlag 1957. 1: Inschrift (Zueignung), S. 339; 2: Inschrift (Zueignung), S. 340; 3: Neunte Elegie, Duino, S. 261; 4: Orpheus-Sonette, 2.Teil Nr. XXIX, S. 301; 5: Inschrift (Zueignung), S. 337; 6: Nachlese aus den Gedichten, S. 316; 7: Nachlese aus den Gedichten, S. 344; 8: Aus dem Stundenbuch, S. 45; 9: Inschrift, S. 341.